BUSINESS ETIQUETTE AND PROFESSIONALISM

Revised Edition

M. Kay duPont,
Certified Speaking Professional
Certified Professional Developement Trainer

A FIFTY-MINUTE™ SERIES BOOK

BUSINESS ETIQUETTE AND PROFESSIONALISM

Revised Edition

by
M. Kay duPont,
Certified Speaking Professional
Certified Professional Development Trainer

CREDITS
Managing Editor: **Kathleen Barcos**
Design and Composition: **ExecuStaff**
Production: **Barbara Atmore**
Cover Design: **Fifth Street Design**
Artwork: **Ralph Mapson**

© 1987, 1993 by Steve Mandel
Printed in the United States of America by Von Hoffmann Graphics, Inc.

CrispLearning.com

02 03 04   10 9 8 7 6 5

Library of Congress Catalog Card Number 97-77676
duPont, M. Kay
Business Etiquette and Professionalism
ISBN 1-56052-475-8

LEARNING OBJECTIVES FOR:

BUSINESS ETIQUETTE AND PROFESSIONALISM REVISED EDITION

The objectives for *Business Etiquette and Professionalism—Revised Edition* are listed below. They have been developed to guide you, the reader, to the core issues covered in this book.

Objectives

❑ 1) **To review business etiquette and its role**

❑ 2) **To discuss techniques for meeting people**

❑ 3) **To discuss telephone and electronic etiquette**

❑ 4) **To suggest good business meeting protocol and multicultural etiquette**

Assessing Your Progress

In addition to the learning objectives, Crisp Learning has developed an **assessment** that covers the fundamental information presented in this book. A 25-item, multiple-choice and true-false questionnaire allows the reader to evaluate his or her comprehension of the subject matter. To buy the assessment and answer key, go to www.CrispLearning.com and search on the book title, or call 1-800-442-7477.

Assessments should not be used in any employee selection process.

ABOUT THE AUTHOR

M. Kay duPont is owner and executive vice president of the Communication Connection, which offers conference programs and training in business relationships, image, success skills, and productive communications. She specializes in helping people build better relationships so productivity and team harmony are higher and more effective. She works with organizations that need to work better together and with individuals who want an edge in the marketplace.

Kay has won many awards for her speaking and training and has earned the prestigious Certified Speaking Professional designation from National Speakers Association and the Certified Professional Development Trainer designation from the International Board of Standards for Training, Performance, and Instruction. For more information, visit Kay's Web page at: www.TCC-WSA.com.

INTRODUCTION

Good office manners may not be listed in your job description, but they certainly play a crucial part in your career. The ability to handle yourself properly today outweighs even your technical skills. If you know what to do, when to do it, and how to do it with grace and style, you'll have a competitive edge in your career. All business experts agree that good manners promote good business.

Why is etiquette so important? Because people judge you and your company by what they see and by what they *believe* to be true. You are never really *you* to other people; you are only the you that they perceive you to be. If they perceive that you're even slightly uncultured or unrefined, your business may suffer. If people perceive you to be a knowledgeable, smooth professional, they'll want to do business with you.

If you questioned all the experts on business manners, each would probably give you a slightly different explanation of what constitutes good behavior in business. Acceptable etiquette even varies from place to place and from person to person. The codes of business conduct in Japan or China differ greatly from those in Alabama or California. Within the United States itself, what is acceptable in New York might be offensive in New Mexico. Even in your own city, an older person might be upset by behavior that would go unnoticed by a younger person. The titles *Mr.* and *Mrs.* or *Ma'am* and *Sir*, for example, annoy some people or seem stuffy, while other people prefer this formality. Some companies encourage the use of first names at all levels of employment, while others find this practice to be unforgivably familiar.

Even so, today's business etiquette is much simpler than it was a few years ago. Terms like *social graces, style, niceties, courtesy,* and *acceptable procedure* help to give us a sense of it. *Etiquette* is defined as "the forms, manners, and ceremonies established by convention as acceptable or required in social relations, in a profession, or in official life." Business etiquette, then, is the way professional businesspeople—regardless of job title or type of business—conduct themselves around others.

Business etiquette relies on tradition, social expectations, and behavior standards. Those things are based on understanding, kindness, courtesy, efficiency, and common sense. What business etiquette boils down to is the new Golden Rule: Do unto others as they would have you do unto them.

"An easy-to-read, informative book that fills a desperate need . . ."

—Letitia Baldrige
America's Foremost
Authority on Manners

CONTENTS

CONTENTS (continued)

S E C T I O N

I

What Is
Business Etiquette?

THE ROLE OF GOOD MANNERS IN BUSINESS

As we become a more high-tech society, the need for a sensitive, personal touch in business increases. As John Naisbitt says in *Megatrends*, "Whenever new technology is introduced into society, there must be a counterbalancing human response." No matter how intelligent or accurate your computer is, you must still interact with other people.

When you use accepted etiquette, you're using the behaviors that encourage human response; you're more likely to get positive results, earn cooperation and support, get commitments, gain clients, and keep peace. You are more likely to succeed when you put that something extra into your way of doing business.

Letitia Baldrige is one of the most respected etiquette experts in the United States. She served in the Diplomatic Corps, and she spent three years as director of staff for Jacqueline Kennedy in the White House. In *Letitia Baldrige's Complete Guide to the New Manners for the '90s*, she says:

> Good manners are cost-effective. They increase the quality of life in the workplace, contribute to optimum employee morale, embellish the company image, and hence play a major role in generating profit. On the other hand, negative behavior, whether based on selfishness, carelessness, or ignorance, can cost a person a promotion, even a job.

A U.S. Office of Consumer Affairs' study revealed some of the costs of poor etiquette. The study showed that "up to 90% of unhappy customers never complain about discourtesy, and up to 91% will never again do business with the company that offended them. In addition, the average unhappy customer will tell the story to at least nine other people, and 13% of unhappy customers will tell more than twenty people."

As Letitia Baldrige comments, "A company becomes a company you want to do business with because of the people who work in it, so business etiquette has a very definite relationship to the bottom line." Good etiquette is good business!

THE ROLE OF GOOD MANNERS
IN BUSINESS (continued)

When viewed in this light, business etiquette is more than which fork to use, or how to smile nicely, or when to wear a tuxedo. Today's business-people must know how to walk into a room full of strangers and feel at ease. They need to be able to introduce themselves and others without feeling apprehensive. They should know when—and how—to make a phone call to cheer or congratulate someone, and when a handwritten note or an e-mail is in order. They must know how to conduct themselves at company social functions and receptions, and understand the complexities of the business lunch.

In this book, we're going to talk about common business situations and the etiquette that applies. Except in the Section IX, Multicultural Etiquette, we'll be talking about American protocol. With our growing global economy, it's not uncommon to be involved with people from all parts of the world, so always remember that other cultures have other customs. Dealing successfully with others takes a smooth stream of communication, free from social misunderstandings that may hinder the accomplishment of our business goals. For an excellent book on understanding cultural differences, read *Working Together* by Dr. George Simons, published by Crisp Publications.

SOME ETIQUETTE BASICS

Holding Doors

Yesterday's etiquette dictated that a man had to back up and let a woman pass through a door first; a younger person had to do the same for an older person. But today's common-sense etiquette dictates that the person in the lead holds the door for the person in the rear. It's that simple.

If people of the same gender approach a door together, the one in the higher position or the one considerably older usually enters first, while the other person holds the door for them.

What about revolving doors? If the woman is in the lead, she enters first and pushes; the man follows and pushes and vice versa. If the person in the rear wants to push a little harder to help out, that's great. The point is not who goes first, but that everyone gets through the doors easily.

Just remember that common sense rules. If someone is carrying an armful of files or packages, the other person takes the lead in all situations, regardless of sex or age.

Train Etiquette

What about the rule that on a bus, train, or subway men or younger people must give up their seats to women or older people? Not any more—unless the people are handicapped or pregnant. Of course, offering your seat is still a nice gesture.

SOME ETIQUETTE BASICS (continued)

Automobile Etiquette

It's nice, but not mandatory, for a man to go around to the passenger side and assist a woman into the car when they travel together. It's especially appropriate when the car is locked. If someone does unlock your door from the outside, please be polite enough to unlock the driver's door from the inside!

Getting out of the car is another story. Some women find it embarrassing for a man to come around and open their car door. What do they do while waiting? If, however, a woman is dressed for a social event and might have trouble maneuvering her dress and wrap, then of course a man should help. If you're a woman with a man who insists on opening your door, good manners dictate that you allow him this tradition without a show of resentment.

It's still good manners for a man to walk a woman to her car if it is parked in a dangerous area; at nighttime, he should accompany her in any area. Of course, it's smart for a man to walk a man to his car as well! And women should always walk into parking lots in groups, if possible.

Elevator Etiquette

Common sense dictates that the people closest to the elevator doors get on first. If you want to be at the front when it's time to get out, go in and stand by the buttons, out of the way. Or go in last. If you're in the very front waiting for your floor, however, you show good manners if you move outside the doors to allow people to exit from the back. Consideration of the entire group should always come before formal etiquette to one person, especially in an elevator!

If you're using the escalator or the stairs instead of the elevator, the man usually follows the woman.

EXERCISE

Take a moment to picture one or two people you see as real professionals—people you look up to. Write their names here and then describe their business etiquette. What do they do in business situations that make them appear professional? What do they avoid doing? List as many behaviors as you can before you go to Section II.

1. Name: _____

2. Name: _____

What do they do?

1. _____

_____

_____

_____

2. _____

_____

_____

_____

Place a check by the behaviors you regularly use.

What do they avoid doing?

1. _____

_____

_____

_____

2. _____

_____

_____

_____

Place a check by the behaviors you regularly use.

S E C T I O N

II

Principles of
Impeccable
Work Behavior

PRINCIPLES OF IMPECCABLE WORK BEHAVIOR

Congratulations! You got the job! Whether you're a new permanent employee or one of America's 35 million contingent workers (temporaries, leased employees, independent contractors, and part-timers), you've just become the "new kid on the block," and people are going to be watching you closely. It's easy to deal with your new coworkers' initial curiosity and, at the same time, establish yourself as a professional in your new position.

Basic Guidelines

The guidelines in this chapter apply to all employees, not just newcomers. Many veteran workers also need to be reminded occasionally of these basic principles of business professionalism.

1. *Be careful with your appearance.* Here are a few general guidelines for the most effective business appearance:

    - *Dress appropriately.* You want to be noticed, but you don't want to stand out. And there are different rules for different situations and work styles. Again, your own organization's style will dictate what is "appropriate."

    - *Dress for the position you want, not the position you have.* Others tend to believe that you are what you appear to be. So when it comes time for promotions, management usually looks first to the people who need the least amount of grooming for the new position.

    - *Dress conservatively.* For most businesses and most business occasions, conservative is best. You will have more credibility in a jacket than without, more credibility in long sleeves than in short, more credibility in conservative colors than in flashy.

2. *Expand your knowledge.* According to a 1988 study by the U.S. Department of Labor and the American Society for Training and Development (ASTD), knowing how to learn is the skill most needed by employees. Learn as much as you can about your job and your manager's job, and how each fits into the organizational structure. Find out what other departments do. Read the trade publication of your industry and profession. Be the one who people turn to for expertise in your area.

PRINCIPLES OF IMPECCABLE WORK BEHAVIOR (continued)

3. *Honor your working hours.* Working nine to five doesn't mean that you arrive at nine and leave at five. It means you *work* from nine to five. Socializing at the coffeepot or eating breakfast at your desk does not constitute working. Five minutes may not seem like much to you, but it may seem like stealing to your manager or CEO, especially in a small or very busy office. Spending 10 minutes on a personal phone call is only a small part of an eight-hour day, but 10 minutes a day equals 50 minutes a week—almost an hour of unproductive time.

If you start getting ready to leave at 4:45, charge out of the office at 4:59, and go screeching out of the parking lot, you'll give the impression that you can't wait to leave—not a very professional attitude. If you cut short a telephone conversation with a customer because it's quitting time, you may lose business.

If you arrive at a meeting late, your actions say, "My time is more valuable than yours; you aren't important to me." Those few extra minutes may make a big difference in the way you're considered for promotions or raises. Be honest. How many hours do you *really* work?

4. *Be friendly.* When you're new, you need people to help you with your new duties, explain procedures, and show you where to get information or material you'll need. Make an extra effort to get along with everyone, but don't try too hard. Ask your new coworkers to have lunch with you; lunch is a great opportunity to get to know each other. Remember that offices work best when individual effort supports the team effort.

5. *Keep personal information to yourself.* Friendliness aside, don't let your life become the office soap opera. When someone asks, "How are you?" don't spill your guts. Some of that information could be used against you later. If you can't control your mood or your mouth, be quiet. The same advice goes, of course, for sticking your nose into others' personal business. Don't. Never discuss or question salary or any other confidential or personal information with coworkers.

6. *Be positive and supportive.* When your day isn't going the way you hoped it would, try to look at the positive side of things—and people. You'll be surprised how quickly you can turn a bad day into a good one. Believe in your coworkers and back them up in public. When your manager makes a decision, give your wholehearted support to it, at least in front of others. Make others look good at every opportunity. Managers, especially, need you to look, talk, write, and act like a positive, supportive representative. Your professionalism reflects on both your manager and your organization.

7. *Keep an open mind.* Make informed judgments, avoid jumping to conclusions, evaluate what you see in addition to what you hear, and don't be a party to gossip. Establishing yourself as a professional means that you show respect for others.

8. *Follow through.* We all get a little tired, especially by late afternoon, but the job you tackle at 5:00 P.M. means as much as the one you start at 8:00 A.M. Cover every angle of a project, and don't wait to be reminded that you need to finish a project. Be accurate. Check and double-check to make sure things are going smoothly and the way you planned. Be realistic about how long an assignment will take, and let others know ahead of time if you anticipate a delay. Set deadlines and meet them.

9. *Communicate.* According to the ASTD study mentioned earlier, only job knowledge ranks above communication skills as a factor for workplace success. Keep people informed in a succinct and useful way. Everyone wants to know what's going on—not every little detail of every day, but what is happening on major projects. Your coworkers want to know about the status of assignments. They want to know immediately about any problems or mistakes. Most of all, if a conflict arises or if someone makes a mistake, remember that everyone is human.

Managers want you, however, to go through the normal channels of communication. Don't go over their heads, and don't bring things to them that don't concern them. If you want to disagree with them, do it tactfully, with a positive alternative, and during a high point in the day.

PRINCIPLES OF IMPECCABLE WORK BEHAVIOR (continued)

10. *Listen.* Speaking and listening are twin skills in communication. Both sides must play a part for communication to occur, and you can learn best by listening to what others know. Ask questions. Hear how other people organize their ideas, how they bring up a new plan, how they respond to changes in procedures. For more on listening, see Section VI.

11. *Solve your own problems.* When you do have to present a problem, bring possible solutions, too. Don't complain about things that can't be changed, and don't blame others when you make a mistake. Accept responsibility when you've made a mistake, and work harder to make sure it doesn't happen again. Learn to accept criticism gracefully without defensiveness.

12. *Work hard.* Be ready and willing. Take on new responsibilities, and do more than others expect. Don't be content to do only what's expected of you or use the excuse that "It's not my job." Look for areas in which you can do more and make yourself more valuable. Volunteer for special projects. Those who wait to be told what to do continue to be told what to do, and their value seldom increases.

13. *Be assertive, but not aggressive.* What's the difference? Assertiveness is appropriate behavior for the situation at hand. It's standing up for your rights without infringing on the rights of other people.

    Aggressiveness is strong, overpowering, often abusive behavior. It's rude, crude, and abrasive.

14. *Don't be in too big a hurry to advance.* Learn as much as you can in the job you have now. Think ahead. Plan. It's like growing up: no matter how eager you are, it takes a certain amount of time. Try to enjoy what you have while it's yours.

15. *Leave gracefully.* If you don't have the job very long, keep your disappointment—or your extreme happiness—to yourself. Just be cordial and say your good-byes quietly. Never bad-mouth the people who have put money in your pocket.

    If someone else is leaving, respect that person's privacy as much as your own. Even if they have resigned, and you can't understand why, respect their opinion. They're still the same people—they just chose not to work there any longer.

EXERCISE

Answer True or False. For those you answer as false, what is the correct answer?

	True	False
1. When a new coworker asks, "Are you dating anyone right now?" you should stalk off, saying, "I don't think that's any of your business."	❏	❏
2. You've been on the job a week and have noticed a good-looking coworker down the hall. You should say something like, "Hey, what's a good-looking person like you doing in this dump?"	❏	❏
3. When someone in your office does something nice for you that you didn't request, you should ask them why they did it.	❏	❏
4. It's perfectly all right to discuss your salary with your coworkers.	❏	❏
5. It's acceptable to come to work late as long as you don't go to lunch.	❏	❏
6. As a temporary employee, you don't have to be concerned about your professional image because you'll only be at the company a few days.	❏	❏
7. A speaker has greater responsibility than a listener in the communication process.	❏	❏
8. The more outgoing you are in the first days of a new job, the more your coworkers will like you.	❏	❏
9. Your new manager will always be happy to answer questions and solve problems for you.	❏	❏
10. When you take a new or temporary job, it's the responsibility of the other employees to make sure you are happy and comfortable.	❏	❏

Answers on page 106.

SECTION

III

Meeting
People

MEETING PEOPLE

You know what they say: A bad first impression is hard to overcome. Accurate or not, that first impression usually lasts. Whether you're a receptionist or a vice president, contact with you may be the only contact a person will ever have with your company. To them, you *are* the company. That's why you should see to it that every visitor to your office gets a cordial yet businesslike welcome.

The way to greet others—not only by what you say, but by your body language—tells a lot about you. Meeting others in a pleasant way and showing sincere interest in them helps produce a favorable first impression.

WHEN YOU'RE THE RECEPTIONIST

Pretend you're the receptionist (or the primary person in a visitor reception area). A visitor comes in. List the first five things you would do.

1. _____
2. _____
3. _____
4. _____
5. _____

If you are greeting people as the receptionist, you don't have to stand and shake hands when a visitor comes into your area. You do have to stop what you're doing, look up, smile, and listen to what the person has to say. If you keep typing or shuffling papers when visitors approach, they will feel that you're not interested in them or their needs.

Don't consider visitors to be an interruption of your work—no matter how much you have to type, no matter how often the phone rings. You should never be too busy to give a visitor a few minutes of your undivided attention.

If someone else in the company needs to come out to greet the guest, call that person immediately and make a brief report to the guest: "Ms. Parkins will be here right away." If Ms. Parkins doesn't come right way, call her back and remind her, and tell the guest that you've spoken to her again and she is coming.

If you need to escort the guests to another area, always take the lead— whether they are older than you or of the opposite gender. It's your office; you're the host. Lead the way, open and hold doors for them, and serve them first if refreshments are being offered.

On their first few visits, guests should always be escorted to their destination within the office. Guests should also be walked back to the main exit at the conclusion of the first few visits, or every time if your office layout is confusing.

Unexpected Guests

What about those guests who don't have appointments—salespeople, for instance? Managers rarely have time for all the people who want to see them. They often don't even have time for the people they want to see. If you, your manager, or your company has a policy about not seeing uninvited guests, tactfully explain the situation to the visitors, ask for a business card, and thank them for stopping by. Be pleasant. Tell them you'll put their card in your supplier file and that, if the need arises, you'll call them. This tells salespeople that you would prefer to call *them* next time. Your politeness keeps your company from getting a reputation as being rude or hard to deal with. If the person calls again (in person or on the phone), explain that their card remains in the file, and suggest that they might want to write to the manager for an appointment.

While They Are Waiting

Sometimes visitors have to wait in your area until their host can see them. That can be uncomfortable for both of you if space is tight. There are a number of ways to make your guests feel more at home:

1. *Always offer refreshments.* If someone came to visit your home, you'd certainly ask, "May I get you something to drink?" Your office visitors deserve the same courtesy.

If you can't leave your desk, get someone to help you, or direct the guests to the kitchen. Or put a coffeepot right out there in the lobby. If you don't have a kitchen or lobby, direct them to the cafeteria or water fountain. But you must mention coffee (or something) to everyone: "Ms. Gonzalez, I'm sorry I can't offer you anything to drink right now. If you'd like some water, there's a fountain just out to the left, and I *can* give you a cup!"

2. *Tell them indirectly where the toilets are located.* Many visitors are embarrassed to ask about the facilities. Be discreet: "If you'd like some water, there's a fountain near the elevator, just to the left of the restrooms."

3. *Be sure they have a chair, an ashtray if smoking is allowed, and current reading material.* Although your annual report is fascinating, guests might also like to read today's newspaper or the current *Business Week*.

WHEN YOU'RE THE RECEPTIONIST (continued)

4. *Show visitors where to hang their coats, or offer to hang their coats up yourself.* Be sure your guests know where you've taken their coats. It's not necessary to help them take off their coats.

5. *Offer as much help as you can*—such as looking up phone numbers.

6. *Maintain a businesslike atmosphere.* When a visitor is near your desk, don't chat with friends or carry on personal telephone conversations. And don't smoke or eat or read when visitors are in your area—even if they do.

7. *Engage in an extended conversation with visitors only if they begin it.* Since they may be reviewing their thoughts before seeing someone, chatting could distract them. If they start a conversation, reply in a friendly, businesslike manner. Be careful not to offer personal information about yourself, your manager, or your company's affairs. If they bring up a controversial theme, it's a good idea to shift the subject.

What if they want to talk and you're very busy? It's not your responsibility to entertain guests (depending on their identity, of course). You've made them as comfortable as possible, and you have work to do. One factor that enters into this situation is the arrangement of your office. Are the guest chairs next to your desk? If the guest seats are across the room, it's difficult for the visitor to carry on a conversation with you.

If you can't do anything about the furniture, be assertive. Answer their questions as simply as possible, smile, and turn immediately back to your task.

WHEN YOU'RE IN AN INSIDE OFFICE

You may need to go out to the lobby to greet guests who have come to see you or your manager. You may skip this courtesy for visitors who come often, but it's a good idea to go to the reception desk to meet all VIPs and first-time visitors.

Make a professional entrance into the reception area. Make sure your posture, facial expression, and body movements are confident and reveal only what will be helpful to you professionally. Don't wear your feelings on your sleeve or allow the stress or disappointment of the day to follow you through the door. If you're negative when you greet people, they will probably reciprocate.

Receiving Guests for Your Manager

Introduce yourself right away: "Good morning, Mr. Widmeyer. I'm Brenda Bones." If you're the host's secretary, add that bit of information: "Good morning, Mr. Widmeyer. I'm Brenda Bones, Ms. Lyndall's secretary." If Mr. Widmeyer doesn't hand you a business card, don't hesitate to ask for it. It will come in handy later, for introductions and for your files. Give the card to your manager as you introduce the visitor, or simply put it on the manager's desk where he or she can see it.

When you show the guest the way to your manager's office, say something like, "Ms. Lyndall is expecting you. Please come with me." Avoid such abrupt commands as "Follow me" or Walk this way."

If you look up and see a person who looks lost, it is certainly good manners to offer to help. But try not to sound suspicious or condescending because they're in your area when they should be in another area. If you suspect that person shouldn't be there at all, call the receptionist and check. If you don't have a receptionist, ask the person politely, "May I help you?" If he or she appears really suspicious, call security.

WHEN YOU'RE IN AN INSIDE OFFICE (continued)

If visitors stop by your desk or poke their heads into your office and ask how to find someone, be polite enough to help. People should not have to wander through your company's or your building's maze. If they're in the wrong department, lead them or carefully direct them to the right department. If they're at the wrong company, help them by checking your building directory, or at least offer to let them use a phone to call their contact and get directions.

When You're the Person Guests Have Come To See

If you, the host, realize you have to keep your guests waiting longer than 10 minutes (which may be poor planning on your part), go out yourself and explain. It irritates people to be kept waiting and have no contact with the person they've come to see. If you need a while longer, give your visitors the option of waiting or returning at another time. If you and your staff are gracious and sincerely apologetic, your visitors' feathers won't be so ruffled when they do see you.

SHAKING HANDS

The professional way to greet someone who comes into your work area is to stand, come out from behind your desk, smile with warmth and interest, and extend your right hand for a firm handshake. If you remain seated while someone is introduced to you, you convey a lack of interest—implying that you'd prefer not to be bothered. (Of course you don't have to rise every time a coworker enters your office, even if your visitor is a woman or someone of slightly higher rank.)

After shaking hands, greet the person verbally by repeating his or her name and immediately stating yours if someone hasn't already introduced you: "Good to meet you, John. I'm Kay duPont."

If you can't shake with your right hand for some reason, offer your left. If you have a permanent disability, you needn't apologize for it. If it's temporary, you need only smile and say something like, "My right hand's a little under the weather right now." If someone asks, make your explanation short and simple.

Your handshake says a lot about you. A firm handshake (without pumping or clutching) shows confidence, warmth, openness, and sincerity; a weak, limp handshake indicates just the opposite. A bone-crusher handshake tells people you're a dominating, insensitive type.

"Pump" the person's hand once or twice (about as long as it takes to say both names), but don't continue to hold on. Even if your introduction continues, let go of the person's hand. Lean forward slightly during the handshake, smile, and make direct eye contact. A handshake without direct eye contact suggests hesitancy, untruthfulness, or a feeling of inferiority.

SHAKING HANDS (continued)

Three Handshake Positions

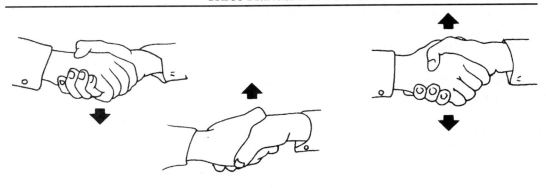

| Taking control | Giving control | Shaking like a professional |

When you shake hands, keep your hand straight, thumb knuckle facing upward. When people turn their hand so their palm faces down in the handshake, it transmits an unconscious feeling of dominance. You appear submissive if you allow the other person's hand to take the dominant position. This submissive handshake is a good one to use when you want to give the other person control or allow them to believe they are dominant.

In business situations, never double-clasp (put your left hand over their right hand), put your hand on their shoulder, kiss (or air-kiss) their cheek, or touch them in any other way. Be respectful of their personality style; not everyone feels comfortable with touching. Hugging and kissing are not done in the office setting, no matter how friendly your group or how close you feel to someone.

There was a time, not too long ago, when the rules of etiquette dictated that a man should wait for a woman to offer her hand first. No longer. Equality governs today: either party may extend a hand first. Even rivals are expected to forgo their competition long enough to perform this small courtesy.

What do you do if you extend your hand and the other person doesn't take it? Simply withdraw your hand discreetly, don't comment, and don't feel any shame or embarrassment.

INTRODUCING PEOPLE

Although we may not be as formal as we used to be, introductions are still very important.

When you introduce someone, start with "Mr. Long, meet Mr. Roscoe from Company/Dept/State," or "Mrs. Brown, I'd like to introduce my son, Cliff. Cliff, this is Mrs. Brown." Never phrase an introduction as a command: "Mr. Roscoe, shake hands with/meet Ms. Long."

Next, say something about the person being introduced: "Ms. Long works in our lingerie division," or "Sally's a former neighbor of ours in Harrisburg." This little bit of information to the group about the newcomer provides a topic of discussion so that the conversation can flow smoothly.

Refrain, however, from long stories about how you met, or about the person's life or background. Avoid phrases of superiority like "Jeff works for me," or "Sally is my girl Friday."

PROPER INTRODUCTIONS

When Introducing	Name to Say First
Younger person to older person (Use younger person's first name, elder's last—about 15 years is the deciding point.)	Older person's ("Ms. duPont, this is Johnny Alexander.")
Peer in your firm to outsider	Outsider's
Nonofficial to official	Official's
Junior executive to senior executive	Senior's
Company executive to customer or client	Client's

INTRODUCING PEOPLE (continued)

Always present the senior citizen, guest of honor, or dignitary first. Be sure to use titles, not first names, when introducing a much older person, a doctor (physician, psychologist, veterinarian, Ph.D.), a member of the clergy, or someone of official rank.

Use a dignitary's title even if that person is retired or no longer holds that position: "Governor Brown," "Mayor Taylor," "Colonel Johnson," "Ambassador Hadham."

When introducing a recently widowed woman, give both her given and her late husband's names: "Mrs. (or Ms.) Greentree, I'd like to introduce my cousin, David Blackwood. David, this is Nancy Greentree. Her late husband, Harry, was a great friend of mine, and Mrs. Greentree founded the Elliot Institute."

An obvious breach of etiquette is calling someone by a name you prefer, not the name they prefer. An unflattering or juvenile nickname has no place in business. If Charles prefers to be called "Charles," that's what you should call him and how you should introduce him—not as "Charlie" or "Chuck." If you don't call him by the right name, or if you mispronounce his name, it's acceptable for Charles to correct you. If Charles prefers to be called "Chuckie," that's his business. Don't assume, however, that you know what people prefer. I use M. Kay duPont as my professional name, and I always present myself as "Kay." I'm continually amazed at the number of people who assume that my first initial "M" stands for "Mary" and bypass "Kay" altogether. They call me "Mary" or "Mary Kay," sometimes even after I've corrected them.

People are very sensitive about their names. Using incorrect names hurts your credibility and your chance of doing business with those you've misnamed.

Being Introduced

When introducing yourself, or when being introduced, always stand and extend your right hand. If the person you're meeting is much older or a higher-level executive, say, "I'm happy to meet you, Mr./Ms. Name," or "How do you do, Mr./Mrs. Name." You may usually call younger people by their first names. If someone says, "How do you do," in response to an introduction, the proper response is, "How do you do" or "Pleased to meet you." "How do you do" is a greeting, not a question.

When Introductions Are Neglected

Far more rude than forgetting a name is not introducing people at all. People are usually very uncomfortable when they're not introduced as part of the group.

When you're expecting several people and they are arriving separately, introduce each person as he or she arrives. Just politely interrupt the group's conversation and introduce the newcomer: "I'd like you all to meet Ann Bradley, with the Communication Connection. Ann, these are our associates from the southeastern office: Susan Starr, Loren Morales, and Fred Farthing."

It's also impolite not to introduce everyone within earshot as you escort someone through your offices. Some people are notorious for introducing visitors to everyone except, say, the secretaries. It's as if the excluded people are invisible. Can you imagine how it makes the staff feel when they're in the group but are passed by?

If you're the one who's not introduced, take the initiative. Don't call attention to the slight, and don't ask for an introduction. Just stand, extend your hand, smile and say, "Hi. I'm Clyde Katte, Ms. Dodge's secretary."

If you are introduced but others are not, you may certainly take the initiative to introduce them if they are standing near you.

If you're in a meeting or at a gathering seated next to a person you don't know, it's perfectly acceptable to start the conversation by introducing yourself.

INTRODUCING PEOPLE (continued)

Saying Good-bye

When escorting your guests back to the main exit, thank them for coming, shake each person's hand firmly, and make good eye contact. Make sure your nonverbals assure them that you heard what they had to say and that your manner conveys your appreciation of their visit.

Just remember that the main rule of good manners in greeting people and making introductions is consideration for everyone. Even if you don't know the precise etiquette, if you put people at ease and show proper respect, your actions will be acceptable.

EXERCISE

Choose the most appropriate answer:

1. You're being introduced to a potential client. Unfortunately, you've been holding a cold drink and your hands are like ice. You

    a. smile and greet the person, but keep your hand at your side for fear he or she will think *you're* cold.

    b. shake, but apologize about your hands, explaining that you've been holding a cold drink.

    c. ask the person if he or she will hold your hands until they warm up.

    d. blow into your palms before extending your hands.

2. Someone has just walked up to you and introduced herself, but you weren't listening very well and didn't get her name. You

    a. don't ask again, because you don't want to look stupid.

    b. ask again, because you don't want to alienate a potential associate.

    c. go find somebody else so he can introduce himself to her and you can listen.

3. You're the secretary for the senior manager in your department. When your manager introduces you to a new secretary, you

    a. smile, remain seated, and wait for the new secretary to extend his or her hand in deference to your position.

    b. stand up and offer your hand.

    c. get up and hug the new secretary to make him or her feel welcome.

    d. explain that you're in charge here, and as long as he or she wants to play by your rules, you'll get along fine.

4. A female manager comes into a male manager's office. He should

    a. rise and greet her.

    b. keep working.

    c. look up and greet her.

    d. stay seated, but enthusiastically say, "Hey, Babe, what's up?"

EXERCISE (continued)

5. You're the receptionist for a small company and have been instructed never to announce an unscheduled visitor without finding out why that person is calling. One day someone walks in without an appointment and asks to see the owner. The visitor gives his name, but won't tell you his reason for being there. You

   a. ask for a business card and let the owner decide.

   b. tell him you'll be glad to tell the owner that he is there if you can tell the owner the nature of his business.

   c. refuse to announce the visitor, telling him you're just following directions.

   d. let him go right in.

6. When introducing your supervisor to a client, you should first say

   a. the client's name.

   b. your supervisor's name.

   c. your name.

7. When being introduced to a woman, is it proper for a man to initiate a handshake?

8. What are two good ways to help you remember someone's name?

9. What's the longest time you can keep someone waiting in an outer office without explanation?

Answers on page 106.

SECTION

IV

Telephone Etiquette

ETIQUOTE

The bathtub was invented in 1850, the telephone in 1875. If you had lived in 1850, you could have sat in the bathtub for 25 years without having the phone ring.

—Jacob M. Braude

TELEPHONE ETIQUETTE

No matter what level you work at in a company, you're likely to use the phone a great deal, so it's vital that you know how to use the phone properly.

Think of all the settings in which you use a phone. You may be using a cellular phone while driving down the highway, or talking to someone in another country or on another continent via your computer, or using a cordless phone while you're filing papers. In any situation, phone courtesy should be automatic.

The problem with telephones is that people can't be impressed by the size of your office, the smile on your face, or the clothes you're wearing. They have only two things to go on—your attitude and your voice. People who call your office only once will base 90 percent of what they think of your company on that one call. Believe it or not, callers can tell whether you're having a good day or a bad day, whether you've had enough sleep—even whether you're sitting up straight—while you talk.

As you read this, you're probably slouched in your chair and your feet may not even be on the floor. Right now, before you move, pretend that your office phone just rang and you're answering it. Say something like "Good morning, the Communication Connection." If you are sitting up straight right now, try slouching just long enough to hear how that phrase comes out. Do you hear how dejected and forlorn you sound?

Now sit up very straight, stretch, take a deep breath, smile, and repeat, "Good morning, the Communication Connection." Isn't it amazing how much lighter and more enthusiastic you sound? Your positive attitude comes across on the phone.

ANSWERING YOUR PHONE

Here are some principles for courteous phone answering. Check those you use.

❑ *Sit up straight, breathe deeply, and smile.* AT&T used to advertise as "the voice with a smile," but such voices are rare these days. Don't feel silly about smiling at a telephone—your voice sounds completely different when you're smiling. After you've reminded yourself to do it a few times, it will come naturally.

❑ *Reach for the pad and pen before reaching for the phone*—unless you're driving or walking. This will enable you to take notes during the conversation to refer to or to pass on to the appropriate party. Start writing as soon as the caller starts talking.

❑ *Answer by the third ring.* Answering promptly lets callers know tht you value their time and don't expect them to wait while you're doing something else. Remember that callers have no way of knowing what you're doing—they only know you're not answering the phone. Quick service helps build a reputation of efficiency for you and your company.

❑ *Identify yourself immediately*—even on your cellular and cordless phones. In the office, give the name of your department and your name: "Book department, Ms. duPont." Identifying yourself eliminates guesswork and saves time. It also promotes callers to identify themselves so you don't have to ask who they are. Even if they don't tell you their names, it becomes less formidable when you have to ask because you've already introduced yourself.

❑ *Be courteous, friendly, professional, enthusiastic, and softspoken.* The principles for telephone etiquette are the same as for business etiquette: use good manners, project good voice quality, treat everyone with respect, and think about what you're saying. Talk into the telephone as you would talk to someone in your office.

❑ *Pay attention.* Callers shouldn't feel that they are competing with other things for your attention. Don't eat or drink or make remarks to people who pass by. If a visitor with an appointment arrives, try to end your conversation or put the caller on hold until you've taken care of the visitor. If you must divert your attention, explain to the caller and put him or her on hold. Don't put your hand over the mouthpiece—it's rude and callers *can* hear you.

❑ *Transfer calls only when necessary,* explain your reasons, and ask permission first. Transferring is one of the most delicate areas of handling telephone calls. When callers are transferred from place to place, their good feelings about your company quickly dwindle. If you can help callers, do so. When necessary, say something like, "I'm sorry, Ms. duPont, I don't have that information. May I transfer you to the accounting department? I'll connect you with Brenda Alexander." Don't just say, "Hang on," and let them go. Some callers may not want to wait because they're too busy to hold. When that happens, say, "I'll be happy to ask Brenda to call you back."

❑ *When you must leave the line, explain why and return promptly with an answer:* "Ms. duPont, I can't locate that information. Where can I reach you so that once I have the information, I can call you back?"

If you must leave the line to answer another line, apologize, letting the first caller know you'll be right back: "Will you excuse me a moment? I have another call I must answer." Tell the second caller immediately that you're on another line and you'll be back as quickly as you can. Even better, offer to call the second person back. The first caller always has priority over the second unless it is an urgent call you must take.

When you return, regain the caller's attention by thanking him or her for holding.

> Don't leave people on hold for more than a few seconds. Letitia Baldrige says, "There is only one thing worse in telephone manners than being put on hold, and that is being put on hold with music playing in the background." It's saying, in effect, that a person will be on hold for a long time, and the music is intended to soothe the savage beast. It doesn't.

❑ *React to the other person's conversation.* Even if you just say, "Yes, I see," or "I agree," at least your caller knows that you're alive on the other end.

❑ *Eliminate as much background noise as possible.* Even though a radio may not bother you, it's magnified on the other end and can be extremely distracting to the caller.

❑ *End the call positively:* "I enjoyed speaking with you, Ms. duPont," or "Thanks so much for your time, Kay. I look forward to meeting you." Then let callers hang up first so you can be sure they have completed their conversation.

WHEN CALLERS ARE DISCOURTEOUS

Sometimes you may have to handle callers who are not as well trained in phone courtesy as you are. Here are some suggestions for courteously handling these callers.

1. *When they talk to others while talking with you.* Suggest a meeting instead—when they aren't so busy. Or ask them to repeat what they said: "Ms. duPont, it's difficult to hear you, if you are addressing me."

2. *When they never seem to get to the point.* Use the direct approach: "Kay, what exactly did you have in mind? How exactly may I help you?"

3. *When they don't even pause to breathe.* Interrupt: "Excuse me, Ms. Neverstop, I don't think I can help you with this. It sounds like you need to speak with our accounting department. Please hold and I'll transfer you to Ben Larson." (Although this breaks the earlier rule about transferring calls, sometimes the situation becomes critical.)

4. *When they run on and on.* Take charge: "Jim, let me summarize what you've said, and then, if there's anything new or different, you can help fill me in."

SCREENING CALLS

In today's hectic business world, it's a fact of life that most executives have their telephone calls answered by their staff. This often makes executives seem inaccessible and puts the staff members in an awkward position.

Because having their calls screened sometimes affects callers negatively, you need to be as tactful as possible. Demanding "Who's calling?" before announcing that the person they want isn't in or isn't taking calls will only irritate callers. If the executive will take calls but wants to know who's on the other end first, try something like "Yes, she's in. May I tell her who's calling, please?" If she's only available to certain people, you could say, "She's away from her office for a few minutes. May I take your name and number and ask her to return your call?" It's just plain rude if the call isn't returned after he or she has been given this information; it tells callers they are considered unimportant.

If the person called is out, you don't need to explain his or her where-abouts. Say something like "Ms. Volcheck is away from her desk. This is Brenda. I'll be happy to try to help you." Never tell callers that someone is out of town unless you know them well. In the first place, it's none of their business; in the second place, you are compromising the home security of the person being called by informing a stranger that their house may be empty.

Never tell a caller anything personal: "I'm sorry, he's in the men's room." "I'm sorry, she just had a baby and had a few complications, so she'll be out for a while." "No, Mr. duPont just got a divorce and isn't feeling well today." Don't laugh—I've heard all of these!

Avoid the phrases "He's not in yet" and "She's already gone for the day." They create a negative perception for the caller. No matter what time of day it is, your coworker is simply "unavailable."

When you need to take a message, get the caller's name, phone number, company name, title if appropriate, action needed, and any additional data that will be helpful in identifying the person or the purpose of the call. A person who can take good messages makes an important contribution to any organization.

SCREENING CALLS (continued)

> Ask your manager to give you a list of people who should be put through without screening—family members, friends, senior management, board members, outside consultants, attorneys. Each morning ask whether anyone special is expected to call that day who needs to be put right through. Also ask for a good understanding of what constitutes an emergency situation and a cause for interruption.

Of course, you'll get to know the voices of many regular callers. When you do, there's no need to ask who's calling or why. Just let your manager know who's on the line.

If you have instructions to find out each caller's business, you might say, "May I tell Ms. Hammond what you're calling about, please?" or "Ms. Hammond is not available at the moment, Mr. Rastow. If you'll tell me what you're calling about, I might be able to help you."

If you phrase your questions politely, most callers will politely answer them. Occasionally, however, you'll get an ill-mannered person who won't answer you. Just use common sense and remember that you're doing your job. If you've been instructed to get the callers' names, you have the right—and the duty—to insist that callers give you their names. Remind them that you're carrying out your employer's orders: "I'm sorry, but Ms. Hammond won't take calls unless she knows who's calling."

What if the caller gives you a name but refuses to tell you a reason for the call? Someone might say, "Kay knows what I want," or "What's it to you?" or even "Never mind who's calling. Just put her on." A good response would be, "I'm sorry, but Ms. Hammond won't take calls if I can't tell her the purpose." Don't be frightened by high-pressure tactics, and don't become rude yourself. Remember that people who really have important business will tell you what they're calling about. Continue to make courteous requests for the information you need.

For more on this topic, see the Crisp Publications 50-Minute book *Time Management and the Telephone* by Dru Scott.

MAKING AND RETURNING CALLS

Whether making or returning a call for yourself or someone else, there are some basic points to remember and adhere to:

1. *Make your own calls.* I know it's prestigious to have someone else dial and hold for you, but it's also rude. When you're very busy, it's acceptable to have your assistant make a call for you and say, "This is Ms. Rogers's secretary at the Communication Connection. Ms. Rogers would like to speak with Mr. Simpson. Is he in, please?" If Mr. Simpson is in, then Ms. Rogers should be on the line when he picks up. It's rude to make a call and say, "Hold for Ms. Rogers," and expect the person called to wait.

2. *Return phone calls within 48 hours.* If you don't, you're offending the person who called you as well as all the people they tell. If suppliers call and you can't use their services, have the manners to call back and say no; don't make them continue to try to reach you indefinitely.

3. *Call only when you have a good reason.* A phone call intrudes into a busy person's day and should not be made without a purpose.

4. *Call only during business hours.* Most people don't appreciate receiving business calls at home.

5. *Plan your calls carefully.* Know whom you want to talk with, and don't call when that person is likely to be out or very busy. Remember to time your calls appropriately for time zones (most phone books have a time zone map).

6. *Be courteous when your call is screened.* There will be times when you won't get right through to someone. Don't let this upset you; it happens to everyone. Explain your business to the staff member, and tell him or her if your message is urgent. Being friendly and honest with the screener usually works in your favor. You also shouldn't ask the answerer, "Who's this?" If you really want to know, try a different tact: "This is Alex Bell. May I ask your name/who's speaking, please?"

MAKING AND RETURNING CALLS
(continued)

7. *Greet the person you're calling politely, identify yourself immediately, and announce your purpose for calling.* Whether it's the first or the 10th time you've called someone, give your name. When you are using a mobile phone, identify yourself and explain that you're on a mobile phone; most of us realize that mobile phone calls are billed by the minute, so your call may be handled quicker.

8. *Be brief; everyone values their office time.* If your call may take a long time, ask whether the caller has time to discuss the matter. If not, set up a specific time to get back with the person. If you're calling someone's mobile phone, be extra brief. Discuss only pressing issues.

9. *Call back if you are disconnected from a call you placed.* It's your responsibility to call back.

10. *Hang up gently.* The last thing callers should hear is their name: "Good-bye, Ms. Donetti." Never slam the receiver in the other person's ear; it's comparable to slamming a door in the person's face.

> The telephone can help you win customers for your company and build a reputation for efficiency and reliability. A solid reputation is important to your company's future—and to yours. Using the telephone to your advantage is really very simple: Just extend the same courtesies you like to receive when you're calling a business office.

EXERCISE

Test your telephone habits by checking the answer that best applies.

	Always	Usually	Seldom
1. I make my own calls and answer my own phone whenever possible.	❑	❑	❑
2. I keep a list of frequently called numbers to cut down on incorrect dialings and save myself time.	❑	❑	❑
3. When calling long distance, I dial direct and stay on the line while my call goes through.	❑	❑	❑
4. When taking or placing a call, I identify myself at the beginning of the conversation.	❑	❑	❑
5. I keep paper or telephone message forms and a pen or pencil by my phone, and I use them.	❑	❑	❑
6. I try to be informative and helpful when taking calls for others.	❑	❑	❑
7. When taking messages, I note the date, time, caller's correct name, caller's number (including area code), the message, and my name.	❑	❑	❑
8. When transferring a call or leaving my phone to get information for the caller, I tell the caller what I plan to do and then place my phone on hold or put the handset down very quietly.	❑	❑	❑
9. I give the caller progress reports on my efforts to find another person or the information requested.	❑	❑	❑
10. I offer to return the call if the caller will have to wait longer than one minute.	❑	❑	❑
11. I speak directly into the telephone, with good enunciation and an appropriate volume.	❑	❑	❑

EXERCISE (continued)

	Always	Usually	Seldom
12. I treat all calls as important and always thank the party for calling.	❏	❏	❏
13. Before leaving my phone, I tell someone where I'm going and when I plan to return so my phone will be covered.	❏	❏	❏
14. I immediately check for messages when I return to my desk, and I return calls promptly.	❏	❏	❏
15. I check the paper roll on the fax machine regularly to make sure senders won't have to resend their faxes.	❏	❏	❏

Answers on page 107.

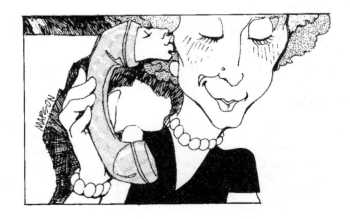

SECTION

V

Electronic Etiquette

ELECTRONIC ETIQUETTE

While today's (and tomorrow's) electronic gadgetry is designed to make the workplace more efficient, it can also cause headaches if not used courteously. The same basic guidelines for the telephone apply here: When in doubt, use common sense and politeness.

FAX MACHINES

Faxes are a critical part of business today, but they should not be invasive. Here are some ideas to remember.

- Fax machines are not in our offices to excuse us from sending letters or making phone calls. Fax machines are best used when time is of the essence.

- Fax machines should not be used for sending advertisements or solicitations. People become annoyed—rightfully so—by unwelcome transmissions.

- If you need to get a message to several people, don't depend on the receiving party to make copies for you. Send a separate fax to each person who needs it. If your message is urgent, mark it "urgent" and call ahead to ask the receiver to be on the lookout. A reminder to receivers: if the fax is marked urgent, deliver it to its intended party as quickly as possible. A reminder to senders: be courteous; don't mark it as urgent if it's not.

- It is proper etiquette for the sender to make sure the fax is received. If you send a fax and don't get a response within the time you think it should take, call the other person and make sure it was received.

- It's a nice idea to send the orginal copy of your message as a backup, although most courts have found faxed documents to be legal and binding.

- If you don't have a plain-paper fax and your office gets long faxes, you can tightly roll the fax the opposite way and secure it with a rubber band or paper clip to straighten it out. That way, when you or someone else opens it, the pages lie flat and can be easily read. If you really want to go the extra mile, unroll the fax after an hour or so, cut the pages, and put them in sequence so you or the intended receiver gets a stack of papers instead of a roll.

- When sending a fax, remember that pencil marks and light inks do not transmit well. Neither do small fonts. Increase your font size to at least 12 points. Many graphics also will not reproduce well, and they take longer to send and receive.

- Cover sheets waste transmission time and paper. There are transmittal notices that stick right on your document (if you're using a hard copy), or you can design your own. If you fax directly from your computer, you can design a simple heading and begin your document a few lines under it.

- Leave your fax machine on when you close your office for the evening. Overseas transmissions come in the middle of the night and on weekends. Check your paper supply each night, too.

Enjoy your fax machine and the time it saves, but always remember that courtesy comes first!

ANSWERING MACHINES

While not the optimal choice for answering your phone, answering machines are still a more satisfactory option than a telephone that is never answered. So here are some guidelines for this necessary evil.

Recording Your Message

- Before recording your final message, practice what you're going to say from a written script. Play it back and keep recording it until you think it's pleasant sounding, enthusiastic, and upbeat. Your message might sound something like this:

   "Hi! This is Kay duPont. I'm not in the office today, but I'm checking my messages and I'll call you back as soon as possible. Please leave your name, your company name, and telephone number when you hear the beep."

   If you're able to say when you'll return, do so.

- Make it clear early on that the caller has reached a machine. Saying, "Hi! This is Teddy," and then pausing may cause the caller to start talking to thin air. A better message is "You've reached ABC Company. No one is available to answer the phone. Please leave your name and number, and we'll return your call as soon as possible."

- Say your name. Simply saying, "I'm not in the office right now," doesn't give your callers the peace of mind of knowing that they have reached the right number.

- Use an unlimited-time tape. If there's little time allowed for a message, the caller may be abruptly disconnected. That's like having someone hang up on you before your business has been concluded.

- Call your own answering machine from time to time. A caller might not tell you that a high-pitched noise comes on the line with your message, or that your message cuts off in midsentence. An unwelcome addition to your message, like interference, should be corrected quickly.

Leaving a Message

- When you leave a message on someone's answering machine, make sure you speak clearly and enunciate well. Saying, "This is Joe at 404-mumblemumblemumble," doesn't help the person return your call. If your name is unknown to the person you're calling, or if it's a hard name to pronounce, be polite enough to spell your name. If you're calling from a company, leave that information as well and carefully pronounce it.

- Always leave your phone number, even when you know the person has it. Speak slowly so your number can be written as the message is being taken off the machine.

- Don't ask people to call you back if you can easily leave the information on the machine. If you just need to tell them that a meeting has been postponed, do so; don't leave a message asking them to return your call just so you can keep playing phone tag.

- Always leave a message on the machine you have reached. If your call isn't important, still have the courtesy to leave your name and say you'll call back later.

VOICE MAIL

Voice mail includes a variety of automated phone answering systems used for customer self-service and for taking messages. The systems' common denominator is that you reach an automated voice that gives you choices of numbers to push on the phone to supposedly get you where you want to go.

Automated Answering Systems

Nine out of every 10 people I talk with hate voice mail, and a recent *communication briefings* survey confirmed that 42% of its readers list automated phone menus as the phone practice that irritates them most.

If you must use an automated system, avoid subjecting callers to a three-minute litany of recorded messages and button pressing. And make sure they can eventually reach a live person. Sometimes callers have questions or needs that just aren't covered in the menu options.

If your company uses voice mail until a representative is free to handle a call, it's a good idea to monitor it, too. Do so at different times of the day to see how long people are holding. The most frustrating thing for callers is experiencing a long delay from the time they are greeted until a representative is available.

When this kind of electronic answering device is used to take incoming calls on non-toll-free lines, customers have good reason to be angry. They are literally paying for this slow, questionable "service."

Also make sure that

   ✔ The message is clear and the voice that delivers it is pleasant.

   ✔ A message comes back regularly to reassure callers while they hold.

   ✔ The electronic music is not abrasive.

   ✔ A real person eventually answers.

   ✔ The caller is thanked for waiting.

E-MAIL

E-mail has become a staple of the workforce. It's quickly being substituted for paper mail at many companies, especially internally. Millions of people have e-mail now, and the average person receives 30–40 messages a day!

In the very near future, e-mail will be an intrinsic part of every business-person's tool chest. And, as with the fax machine, we'll wonder how we ever survived without it.

While it increases productivity, however, e-mail should never replace those critical interpersonal skills. It's very poor etiquette to fire someone, deliver bad news, or discuss emotional issues through e-mail.

E-mail also increases the danger that we may move too quickly. The speed of sending a message, combined with the lack of body language, expression, and tone that reveal emotion in regular conversation, require restraint and control. E-mail is not the proper forum for venting personal criticism or dashing off hasty notes.

Think about who may read your message—not only who the message is for, but also whoever else who may read it. Would you say to this person the same thing you're writing? Have you inadvertently been sarcastic or judgmental? Is the receiver someone who's sure to put a negative spin on your message? If so, use the phone or meet in person instead. Why risk creating anxiety or even distrust by sending messages that lack warmth?

Netiquette

Just as with all other forms of communication, there are rules of *netiquette*, or e-mail etiquette. Whether you're responding to internal company e-mail or posting replies to a public bulletin board, mind your manners:

▶ **Be informal, but polite.** E-mail is more like conversation than letters, memos, or faxes. But you don't have any of the cues (voice inflection, facial expression, gestures) available to convey shades of meaning that you do when you talk face-to-face. It's quite easy to start a misunderstanding telectronically.

E-MAIL (continued)

► **Don't use all uppercase letters.** You can occasionally use uppercase letters to highlight items when you want special ATTENTION drawn to them, or you can set a word off with **asterisks** or <<brackets>>. But use caps sparingly. Many new users of electronic services leave their Caps Lock on. In the electronic world, this is the equivalent of SHOUTING! It's tiresome to read, and it eliminates the availability of caps to show emphasis when you need it.

► **Humor helps.** As with any communication, humor can help too. If your message is fun to read, people will be more likely to remember it. Just know that some humor that works face-to-face doesn't work in e-mail. And sarcasm almost never works in this medium. If you do make a joke, or are being lighthearted, you can use comments like <grin> or <groan> to add clarity.

► **Be polite.** Avoid starting a message with something like "Why haven't you answered my questions?" You'll do more for the relationship if you open with a face-saving statement: "I wasn't sure if my message got through yesterday, so here it is again." Electronic messages that begin with "Why didn't you" come across as even more directing and authoritative than when you talk on the phone or in person. Especially if you give in to the temptation to use all caps!

Keep in mind that readers will respond more willingly if you remember the human element. Add a personal line or two when you know the reader well, and remember the words *please* and *thank you*. The medium may be new, but the messages are tried and true.

► **Make sure your message is clear.** Have you written clearly and concisely all that the reader needs to know? Or have you withheld details so the person has to read between the lines or assume?

► **Get to the point, and don't write too much.** Overloading readers with unrelated or unnecessary details, or giving them information in a rambling order, keeps them from easily figuring out what's important and what's not.

► **Don't overuse e-mail.** Avoid cluttering people's valuable electronic space with nonurgent items that you could fax or send by regular "snail" mail. Don't assume that people you communicate with aren't up to speed on the latest news and trends. They may think you're patronizing them if you send nonrelevant information.

EXERCISE

Answer True or False. For those you answer as false, what is the correct answer?

	True	False
1. The fax machine is the best way to send out long promotional pieces to prospective customers.	❏	❏
2. When you need to send a fax to several people, you should just send a cover sheet and ask the receiving office to make copies for everyone.	❏	❏
3. It's not necessary to say your name on your office answering machine or voice mail; "Please leave a message" is good enough.	❏	❏
4. When you're the caller, it's not necessary to leave your phone number on someone's machine or voice mail if you know the callee already has it in their records.	❏	❏
5. It's OK to hang up when you reach a wrong number.	❏	❏
6. Everybody likes voice mail systems.	❏	❏
7. Your voice mail message should be cute and bouncy.	❏	❏
8. E-mail should be more formal than other means of communication.	❏	❏
9. Typing e-mail messages in all caps makes them easier to read.	❏	❏
10. You don't need to respond to e-mail messages as quickly as to voice mail.	❏	❏

Answers on pages 107–108.

SECTION

VI

Planning and Attending Business Meetings

PLANNING MEETINGS

Businesspeople attend billions of meetings each year. The cost of these meetings is staggering. Even the cost of conducting a day-long meeting with 10 staff members is high. In addition to the meeting room, coffee, meals, travel, and audio-visual equipment, you have to add the cost of staff members pulled away from their jobs. For this reason alone, meetings need to make good use of everyone's time. For a comprehensive book on planning, running, and evaluating business meetings, see the Crisp Publications 50-Minute book *Effective Meeting Skills* by Marion E. Haynes.

Who Should Attend?

The purpose of the meeting determines who the participants will be. If the meeting is to provide information or ask for a vote on a previously discussed issue, the number of people attending usually presents no problem. If the meeting's objective is to study problems or examine issues and calls for analytical and synergistic decision making, the meeting may be more successful if you limit the number of attendees.

Once you determine how many will attend, it's wise to consider who should be invited before issuing invitations. When you have any doubt, meeting experts suggest excluding people rather than including them. You need to have the "right" people—those who *must* be there, not those who should or could be.

Give your in-town guests a minimum of 48 hours' notice, and give your out-of-town guests at least two weeks'. If people are coming from out of town, include directions for driving or for getting from the airport to the meeting facility.

Even if the meeting location is familiar, people still need specific details on the invitation, like building number, floor, room or suite, and starting and ending times. Be sure to list a central telephone number to serve as a message center for participants, and mention appropriate dress for the occasion.

PLANNING MEETINGS (continued)

Where Should It Be Held?

Real estate agents believe location is everything. In planning meetings, location is also a crucial decision, and the purpose should determine the place. Can you meet in your office? Which room? What is the most central off-site location? Do you want the atmosphere to be social or businesslike? What should the meeting facility offer? What should be the layout for the meeting room?

Consider the room size in conjunction with the number of people attending. A few people sitting in a large room can make the group feel uncomfortable. Too many people in a small room will produce a stuffy, claustrophobic feeling. How well the room is filled also affects the acoustics.

Conference-Table Seating

The chairperson should always sit at the head of the table. You can easily indicate where the head of the table is: blackboards, easels, and screens should always be behind, or slightly to one side of, the head of the table, and the main door should face the chairperson.

Officers of the organization and other participants who will be addressing the group should sit to the right and left of the chairperson. If you plan a discussion format with no specific presentation, let the participants choose their own seats.

ATTENDING MEETINGS

Promptness

It's always bad manners to arrive late for a meeting—any meeting. In fact, you should plan to arrive a little early! If you are unavoidably detained, call and tell your host how soon you'll arrive. If this is impossible, apologize when you arrive and hope for the best.

> How long should you wait for someone when you have an appointment? Ten minutes is too long to keep someone waiting, but sometimes people do get involved in other business and forget they have visitors in the lobby. So, after about 10 minutes, check with the receptionist or secretary. If you need to leave, write a message on your business card and leave it for the person: "Sorry. Had to get to another appointment. I'll call you this afternoon and see if we can reschedule."

Greetings

When the host or a representative comes out to greet you, or you reach the meeting room or host's office, extend your hand in a firm handshake. If there's a group in the room, try to shake hands first with the senior or most influential person in the group or the person you made the appointment with. Wait for your host to indicate a chair for you to sit on. Then sit comfortably, but erect and poised, with both feet on the floor, and don't fidget. Put your briefcase or purse on the floor. (See Section III for more on entrances and exits, shaking hands, and making introductions.)

It's not necessary to rise each time a peer enters. If the group starts to rise from their seats as you enter, you can simply acknowledge the courtesy with a smile, or say, "Please keep your seats."

When you are the meeting leader, start with a couple of minutes of small talk, then get down to business. When you are an attendee only, wait for the leader to begin the discussion.

ATTENDING MEETINGS (continued)

Honoring Territory

According to many studies of nonverbal behavior, humans are territorial. Robert Ardrey, author of *The Territorial Imperative,* says we humans mark our spaces with our belongings, and we have a "comfort zone" we don't like others to enter without being invited. People who share a table or office unconsciously draw a line down the middle and stake out their side of the table. People who move into other people's space may be rebuffed for invading a private zone.

If you take up too much space in a meeting, you'll be considered rude. If you move chairs or other furniture to give yourself more space, those whose space you move into won't like it. It may also be considered an intrusion to look for something on someone else's desk, or to use a person's belongings without permission. It's one thing to handle someone else's pen or notebook when asked; it's quite another to take liberties on your own.

If you lean too far into someone's comfort zone, you'll probably be resented (particularly in male-female encounters). In America a safe distance is about three feet. More than five feet, however, may be considered too "distant."

To honor people's territory during a meeting, pass out copies of your presentation so everyone can read it in his or her own territory. And don't put your copy—or any other papers, files, or personal belongings—on your host's desk or chair. Keep your things in your lap or on the floor beside you.

Keep Your Clothes On

Do not remove your suit jacket or loosen your tie unless the host or hostess does so or specifically makes the suggestion. If you do remove your jacket, don't put it on another chair; keep it with you.

Position Yourself

Sit with good posture, relaxed and comfortable, leaning toward the person you're doing business with. It also helps to know where to sit. In a meeting of only two people, you want to be to the other person's right side, not directly across the desk from them, with a moderate amount of space between you. Think about being someone's "right-hand man." When talking with two people or more, position yourself to see the reactions from all parties—at the end of the line or across from them all and slightly to the right side of the group leader. If you're a junior member of the group, however, you have to take your lead from the others. After you've been signaled to a seat, say, "Thank you," and go quickly.

If you're in a meeting with people you'd rather avoid, don't sit directly across from them—it's too symbolically confrontational. Choose a seat on the same side of the table, with one or two allies between you.

Listen

Listening to other people and being interested in them is one of the great keys of etiquette and diplomacy and the greatest compliment you can pay to another person. Some executives say they can actually tell whether people have been listening by the quality of the questions asked during a meeting. Your listening habits certainly become clear if you're required to make a summation of the speaker's main points at the meeting's end.

Proper listening etiquette includes responding with appropriate facial expressions and body movements: leaning forward, moving closer, being attentive, showing interest. Smile or frown, as the speaker does. Encourage people by asking appropriate questions. Don't finish someone's sentences, and always allow them to finish their idea before replying. If you don't understand something, ask questions to clarify.

When you don't agree, let the person finish, then try to summarize what you heard to make sure you've received an accurate message. Then state your viewpoint calmly and rationally.

Never interrupt. Interrupting stops the listening and evaluation process, and it's the worst kind of rudeness. For more on listening skills, see the Crisp Publications 50-Minute book *The Business of Listening* by Diane Bone.

ATTENDING MEETINGS (continued)

When Guests Arrive

In the business world, we still show deference to visitors, people in management, and our elders. We should begin doing this at an early point in our careers and continue even when we merit such respect ourselves!

When a guest from outside the company comes into the meeting room or joins the table, the company people should rise and properly greet that person. When more senior members of management arrive, junior executives should rise and shake hands with them. This holds true whether the meeting takes place in a conference room, a restaurant, or the junior manager's office (unless the appearance is routine). See Section III for the rules on greeting and introducing people.

Leaving the Meeting

If you are the one who called the meeting, you are responsible for ending it. Watch your host's time; don't take more than you asked for. When you have completed the meeting, stand, shake hands again, and leave with authority. If the meeting takes place in your office, walk your guests to the door.

If you were invited to the meeting, wait for the host to announce or indicate the meeting's end. Then pack up your belongings, thank people individually, shake hands, and leave gracefully. (If the meeting was with your manager or a higher executive, a handshake may be inappropriate unless you have just renegotiated your job responsibilities, talked about increasing your salary, or received a promotion.)

Remember to take any materials you received during the meeting, as well as notepads, pens, or any other items you brought with you. Leave the room with your head and shoulders erect and confident, but also relaxed.

MEETING TRIVIA

Office meetings use 35–40% of the U.S. manager's working day.

Eleven thousand meetings are taking place in America right this minute.

EXERCISE

Answer True or False. For those you answer as false, what is the correct answer?

	True	False
1. The first step in planning your meeting is to decide where to meet.	❑	❑
2. It's never necessary for a man to stand when a woman enters his office.	❑	❑
3. A married couple should always be seated next to each other at a business function.	❑	❑
4. Twelve hours' notice is enough for a company sales meeting with out-of-town reps.	❑	❑
5. The head of the table always faces the door, if possible.	❑	❑
6. You should never burden the receptionist in your host's office about little things like hanging up your coat or directing you to the restroom.	❑	❑
7. When you enter someone's office for a meeting, always choose the chair closest to the door.	❑	❑
8. If you need to spread out your paperwork, do so on the corner of your host's desk.	❑	❑

Answers on page 108.

SECTION

VII

Planning and Attending Meal Meetings

PLANNING MEAL MEETINGS

The business world has grown so complex that executives expand their visibility by becoming involved with community groups and charities—and their lunches and banquets. Food and business cannot be separated anymore!

When a meal meeting is your responsibility, your involvement depends on the number of guests, the elaborateness of the meal, and how much planning the restaurant, hotel, or club will help you do. Much of your job as meeting planner is common sense. You can simply use many of the principles you would apply for a dinner party at home, and make them more appropriate for business.

If you choose to have your meeting at a restaurant, remember that the facility you select will be seen as an extension of your office. If you're taking one person to lunch, take that person's tastes into consideration. If you're planning a larger meeting, choose a facility where the food is good and the service is reliable.

If you often take people to lunch or dinner, it's good practice to become a regular at one or two restaurants so that you and the staff understand and respect each other's needs. Another advantage is that most guests are impressed when the maitre d' calls you by name and leads the party to your favorite table.

Call your contact at least two weeks before a function, and make the reservation in your name and the name of your company. Let the restaurant know how many will be in your party. You might want to ask for a remote table or a private room. If you intend to pay with a credit card, make sure it will be honored. It's even better if you can arrange to be billed for the meal so you won't have to deal with it at the table. Verify your arrangements the day before your meeting.

PLANNING MEAL MEETINGS (continued)

When you arrive at the facility (before the others, of course), recheck your reservations (and your menu if you've preordered), and give the maitre d' an impression of your credit card so there will be no confusion at the table about who is paying. Wait in the lobby to great the others; if there is no lobby, go to the table, but keep a close watch for the others. How long should you wait for a luncheon partner? Call the person's office about 15 minutes after the assigned time. If the office doesn't know why the person hasn't arrived, wait 15–20 minutes more. Then either order or leave.

Make sure there's a place for coats nearby so they are safe during the meeting and people can easily pick them up afterward. As host, you should pay the coat-check fee, with an appropriate tip.

If someone arrives wearing an expensive coat, don't insist on checking it for them. If others are checking theirs, say something like "Would you prefer to keep your coat with you?" Then you can help remove the coat, if appropriate. One of you should then put the coat on the back of the owner's chair.

If you and your guests are being led into the dining room by the maitre d', your guests should precede you. If you're seating yourselves, take the lead. Be sure to offer the "power seat" at the head of the table to your guest of honor. Seat yourself with your back to the door or main part of the room.

If you're a man meeting with a woman, it's still polite (but not mandatory) to hold her chair as she is being seated (if the maitre d' has not done so). You do not, however, have to rise each time she leaves or returns to the table.

Let the servers know you're the host. If possible, introduce yourself ahead of time; if you can't, let them know through eye contact and assertiveness. When asked if you would like drinks or appetizers, repeat the question to your guests to establish your position. Or, just to establish position, take the lead and say, "I'm going to have a glass of wine. What would you like?" If the server asks for your order before your guests' orders, say, "Please take my guests' orders first."

Head Table Seating

When there are several tables involved, you may want to set your room with a head table for dignitaries. If you're honoring too many people to fit at one head table, set up a second. Place this table in front of, and lower than, the main table. (The main table, of course, will have to be on a riser.) If a second head table can't be arranged, use honor tables, placed adjacent to, or just in front of, the head table. Placeards or tent cards may be used to indicate seating.

Guests at the head table are usually seated in this way (if you're looking toward the audience): The presiding officer sits to the right of table center (or the lectern) if the number of guests is even; in the center if the number is odd. The person with the highest rank sits to the right of the presiding officer, next highest to the left. The others alternate right and left according to rank. Those guests at the head table who have no official rank (such as the invocator) sit at the ends.

The presiding officer should introduce the guests seated at the head table in descending order of rank.

The seating arrangements for a regular table replicate those for conference room seating (see below). If you can't easily identify the head of the table, put the dignitary farthest away from the kitchen, facing the main entrance, if possible. Husbands and wives are not normally seated together at a formal dinner.

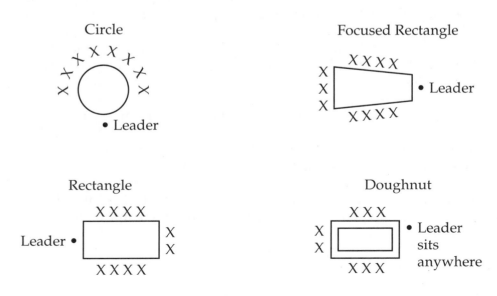

Circle

Focused Rectangle

Rectangle

Doughnut

PLANNING MEAL MEETINGS (continued)

Menu

When planning a menu, always consider various tastes and foods that may be unacceptable because of religious or other beliefs. Chicken is fairly safe, but certainly not the only choice. It is a good idea to offer a vegetarian choice of entree. Most hotels and caterers are accustomed to meal meetings and offer other selections. You might also distribute a menu to participants beforehand with a notation that the facility can substitute entrees if notified by a certain time.

It's never a good idea to serve alcoholic beverages during lunch. It's also not a good idea to serve alcohol at a dinner meeting until the speakers have completed their presentations, although many businesses do. At large dinner meetings, entertainment is often provided after the keynote speaker, and this is a much more appropriate time to serve alcoholic beverages. It is best to check your company's usual practice and follow it.

Conversation

Relax for a few minutes before the meal with small talk, but avoid personal topics. Don't talk about your health or anyone else's. Don't ask questions about spouses or live-ins, especially to associates of the opposite sex. Avoid ethnic subjects, religion, and politics. World news is appropriate; so is your business or another guest's business (never the business of someone not there). You may also ask about the well-being of common acquaintances.

Be careful with your compliments as well; personal comments may be perfectly acceptable to people you know, but they could be misconstrued by new acquaintances.

Remember that revealing confidential information, using insensitive humor, making sexist remarks, and berating your company or its staff are definite career killers. If alcohol affects your judgment in conversation, stick to mineral water at business events.

If you must interrupt a conversation, wait for a break in the intensity. Make eye contact and say, "Excuse me," when you must interrupt or leave the table or group.

If time permits, save your business discussion until after the meal. If that's not feasible, don't allow your business to be interrupted by servers; work out an agreement with the maitre d' ahead of time so that servers approach only at your signal.

> Never use dead-end questions like "How are you?" or "How's the weather?" or "Is it still snowing?" to begin a conversation. Questions that elicit one-word responses create awkward silences. If you want to invite conversation, try asking *who, what, where, when,* and *why* questions. Then listen. If you asked the questions, the least you can do is listen to the answers.

Paying the Bill

The check can be an embarrassing challenge, especially for a female host. The rule is quite simple: The one who did the inviting does the paying. The best way to handle this situation is to arrange the details with the maitre d' before the others arrive.

It's appropriate to motion to the server to bring your bill, or to ask for it when you're finishing the meal. If the server hasn't figured out who's in charge and puts the bill in the middle of the table, pick it up immediately without comment. Also avoid commenting about the total, although you may silently verify the figures if necessary to determine accuracy of the amount and the tip.

If you received the bill on a tray, look at the bill and replace it face down on the tray with your credit card or money on top. If the bill came in a folder, put the card or money into the folder, with the tip showing above the folder, and leave it on the table. If the restaurant is extremely busy, or if the server doesn't return for the folder within a couple of minutes, go ahead and put your payment on top of the folder. It's not as proper, but sometimes it's quicker!

PLANNING MEAL MEETINGS (continued)

Tipping

Confident tipping—without fuss or comment—can make you and your guests feel more comfortable. Tipping has become a customary part of business life, although it is still theoretically optional. Leave a tip to show your appreciation for the service you received, not just because you're supposed to. Don't reward poor service but, no matter how bad the food or service, never make a scene during your meeting. Bring any problems up later with the manager, or write a polite letter outlining precisely why the food was unacceptable or the service poor. Always report unpleasant experiences; if you don't, management can't correct the problem.

A tip should be based on the amount before tax and should not be added if a service charge has already been added to your bill. As an ultimate tip, also inform the server's employer of excellent service.

Tipping should be done quietly. Hand cash to the maitre d' or wine steward, leave cash or the credit card slip on the table for your server. Think about your tipping money ahead of time; carry small bills in a special pocket so you don't have to leaf through your wallet. See the following Tipping Table for guidelines.

Tipping Table

Airport		Hotel	
Bus driver	6–10% of fare	Doorman	$1–$2 per use
Car-rental shuttle driver	$1–$2	Bell staff	$1 per bag
Curbside baggage handler	$1 per bag	Housekeeper	$1–$2 per day
Limousine driver	15% of fare	Room-service server	15% of bill unless included
Taxi driver	11–15% of fare	Shuttle driver	$1–$2 per use
		Parking valet	$1–$2 per use
		Bartender at reception	50¢–$1 per drink
		Banquet captain at a convention	$20–$50

Tipping Table (continued)

Expensive Restaurant		Modest Restaurant	
Maitre d'	$2–$5	Maitre d'	N/A
Table captain (who supervises servers assigned to your table and attends to any complicated service)	5%	Table captain (who supervises servers assigned to your table and attends to any complicated service)	N/A
Server	15–25%	Server	10–20%
Wine steward	$3–$5 per bottle or, in a very posh restaurant, 11–15% of the cost of the wine	Wine steward	N/A
Bartender	15–20% (minimum $1)	Bartender	15–20%
Washroom attendant	50¢–$1 per person using the facility	Washroom attendant	N/A
Coatroom attendant	$1 per coat	Coatroom attendant	50¢–75¢ per coat
Doorman	$1 for summoning your car or taxi	Doorman	N/A
Garage attendant	$1–$2	Garage attendant	50¢–$1

ATTENDING BUSINESS MEALS

The business meal, no longer limited to lunches, has become standard operating procedure in America. And you must be as sharp and professional at a meal function as you would be in the boardroom, maybe even more so. In the boardroom, at least, you don't have to worry about which spoon to use!

There's a story in the personnel field about a very successful business owner who always managed to hire top-notch, long-term managers. He once told an interviewer that before he would hire a manager to work for his company, he would invite that person to lunch. If a person salted the food before tasting it, he or she lost the job. "Lack of manners and stuck in a rut," the owner said.

Times haven't changed much. The social atmosphere of breaking bread together reveals a great deal about your ability to relate to others and whether you can be trusted with responsibility.

Breakfast Meetings

The workday is getting longer in most organizations, but instead of going later, it's starting earlier. The power lunch of the early '90s has been replaced by the in-house company breakfast meeting. Breakfast at the conference table is the hottest office gathering place since the water cooler. Caterers nationwide are adding to their morning staffs to meet the demand for dawn (6:30–8:00) breakfasts of the corporate team, and many report that breakfast orders have doubled in the past 10 years.

The working breakfast is born of the same time pressure that has shrunk the lunch hour to an average of 29 minutes. With so much work to be done, going to and from a restaurant is a waste of time for many businesspeople.

For time-conscious people, the breakfast meeting is perfect. But few meetings are as hard on attendees—especially those like me whose hearts don't really beat with conviction until after noon. To avoid this, prepare ahead of time. Do all your paperwork the night before, and make sure you know the exact location of everything you'll need (including the car keys and the restaurant). Lay out your clothing, and check for spots and wrinkles. Polish your shoes. Set the alarm for a little earlier; you may be moving slower than usual.

Listen to the news as you dress. Read the front page and the business section of the paper too. You can be sure that any morning person knows the latest information!

When you order your meal, think twice about messy foods like jelly dough-nuts or soft-boiled eggs or bacon. They don't look good on your tie and don't sound good in your mouth.

Table Manners

In most restaurants, your napkin will be either in your glass, in your plate, in front of your plate, or to your left. Put it in your lap as soon as you're seated, or as soon as the host does if you're a guest. At formal restaurants, the server will remove your napkin from its place and put it across your lap. Just quietly say, "Thank you." You may tuck the napkin into your belt (but not your collar!) if you think it will help you keep stains off your clothing. If you need to leave the table, put your napkin on the right-hand side of the table next to your plate or on the back of your chair, and put it back in your lap when you return.

When you're the host, you should order and be served last. Allow your guests to read the menu, and offer suggestions only if asked. When you're a guest, you may order whatever you wish, as long as it's not the most expensive item on the menu. Don't order seconds of anything—including drinks. It's rude to spend someone else's money without permission. (If this does occur, the host has every right to override the offender, usually with the excuse of time.) Remember that you may unobtrusively change or cancel an item after everyone else has ordered.

In most American restaurants, your food will be served from the left and cleared from the right. Expect the server to reach over your shoulder, and lean slightly as this occurs. In international restaurants, servers will clear your bread plate and knife from your left instead. I have been at many restaurants, however, where they serve from the right and clear from the left. In fact, some restaurants seem to have no rule at all! Many servers justify this by saying that they will serve and clear from whichever side seems to interrupt the diners least. Good thinking, if you ask me! Just be aware that the servers are trying to do their job, and try to get out of their way as discretely as you can.

ATTENDING BUSINESS MEALS (continued)

Like Mother taught you, keep your elbows off the table while eating, but you may rest your forearms there between courses. What you don't do between courses in America is smoke!

As you eat, use your silverware from the outside in (see figure below). The restaurant places it in that order for your convenience. Bring the food to your mouth, not your mouth to the food. When you finish with a utensil, use the resting position and finished positions shown below. A used piece of silverware should never be put on the table.

Using Utensils

Use utensils from the outside and work your way in.

The rest position tells the waitress that you're still eating.

The finished position tells the waitress that you're finished.

Helpful Hints

- Scoop your soup away from you.
- Use your knife and fork to cut large, flat pasta such as lasagna; use your fork and spoon to swirl long, string pasta such as linguini (a small amount).
- If you have a shrimp cocktail, use your cocktail fork to hold your shrimp and take bites of it, rather than cutting.
- Use your knife to cut fruit from the core and your fork to bring the pieces to your mouth.
- When eating shellfish, hold the shell with your hand and eat the meat with a cocktail fork. Do not stack the shells.
- When eating steak, cut and eat one piece at a time.
- Use your knife and fork with lamb or pork chops.
- Cut or pull chicken off the bone with your knife and fork, then cut it into bite-sized pieces.
- Cut off the tail and head of a whole fish, cut along the backbone, fold the meat back, remove the whole skeleton and set it aside before you begin eating. You may ask the server to do this for you.
- Vegetables served in side dishes can be eaten out of the dish or placed on your plate.
- Never leave your spoon in the cup or soup bowl after using it. Put it on the saucer.
- To eat strawberries, hold them by the stem.
- Raw apple pieces may be eaten with your fingers.
- At a clam bar, it's acceptable to suck the clam off the shell. At a restaurant, use a fork for the clam, a spoon for the broth.
- You may spread cheese with either a fork or a knife.
- You may sip your coffee or tea with a spoon when it's too hot to drink normally.
- You may eat the green "fat" from a lobster.
- Fruit pits go untouched from mouth to spoon to edge of plate.
- After using sugar out of a packet or butter off a paper square, put the paper under the edge of your plate, on the edge of your butter plate, or in the ashtray if nobody's smoking.
- Use a spoon to get jam from a jar, then put it on your butter plate. Use your knife to put it on your bread.
- Eat artichoke leaves with your fingers.
- You may eat firm asparagus with your fingers at an informal dinner.
- It's not necessary to cut olives or cherry tomatoes before eating.
- You may drink your soup if it's served in a cup with handles.

ATTENDING BUSINESS MEALS (continued)

When you need to pass items around the table, always pass them to your guests first, to your right. If you are asked to pass the bread or rolls, pass the butter as well. When the butter comes to you, place a small amount on your bread plate. If you don't have a bread plate, put the butter on the edge of your dinner plate. Break your bread into small pieces and butter it one bite at a time, keeping the pieces on your bread plate or on the table next to your forks. If the server places coffee or tea on the table without pouring it, the person closest to the pot should offer to pour. You may reach for anything within easy reach, but not across the table. Never push your plate toward the center of the table when you've finished.

Excuse yourself for all biological functions, including blowing your nose. Blowing your nose on the restaurant's napkins—paper or otherwise—is very bad form. So are using a toothpick and putting on lipstick at the table.

Sometimes you may want to offer a toast for a job well done or for a special event. If so, follow the KISS rule: Keep It Short, Simple, and Sweet. "Roasts" are usually no fun for the person honored. If you're the person being toasted, don't rise or drink to the toast until the toasters are finished. If you're a nondrinker, just raise an empty glass or a glass of soda.

Thank-You Notes

Whether you were invited to breakfast, lunch, tea, dinner, or a reception, always send your host a handwritten thank-you note.

Can You Refuse?

Sure, as long as you're willing to face the consequences. Many people consider a business meal a waste of time, but the choice is yours. If your manager asks you, you probably should go. If suppliers ask, you have every right to tell them that your decision in no way affects your doing business together, but you prefer not to be entertained by vendors.

EXERCISE

Answer True or False. For those you answer as false, what is the correct answer?

	True	False
1. You and your manager are supposed to go to a business luncheon together with several good clients. You've arrived, but your manager has not. When the clients start to order alcoholic drinks, you should order a drink, because it won't look good to be out of sync with your clients.	❏	❏
2. Glasses of white wine should be held by the bowl, not the stem.	❏	❏
3. It's never acceptable to sip your coffee or tea with a spoon.	❏	❏
4. As host at a business meal, you should place the highest-ranking guest on your left.	❏	❏
5. When meeting a client for a meal, always wait for your guest in the bar or at your table.	❏	❏
6. When a woman invites her male client to discuss business over a meal, the man should always pay.	❏	❏
7. When a man and a woman are escorted to a dining table, the man immediately follows the maitre d'.	❏	❏
8. You should always take the first roll from the basket and then pass to your guests.	❏	❏
9. You should always tip your servers at least 10%.	❏	❏
10. You must cut the olives and cherry tomatoes in your salad before eating them.	❏	❏

Answers on pages 108–109.

S E C T I O N

VIII

Business Invitations and Gifts

SENDING INVITATIONS

The most important rule in sending invitations is to understand your guest. Take into consideration the kind of relationship you have with this person and what he or she likes to do, and extend your invitation accordingly.

Inviting Your Manager

It's not usually proper for a junior person to invite a manager to dinner, unless you have become social friends. If you've been entertained in your employer's home when other people were also invited, don't feel compelled to return the invitation. If you do want to entertain your manager and you're even the least bit hesitant about doing so, it may be better not to entertain at your home. Many people are uncomfortable with their employer in a private setting, and dinner at home is no time to try to create rapport. It's also hard to judge whether you've overdone or underdone your entertainment. Never invite your manager to your home strictly because you think it will help your career.

Inviting Another Executive

What if two executive couples want to get together for an evening? Should the wife of one call the wife of another? What if the executive *is* the wife? Actually, if the spouses don't know each other, it might be more appropriate just to have lunch! But sometimes it's a nice career booster to invite another business associate for a social evening. Of course, the spouse must always be invited, especially if the event occurs on a weekend. If you invite an associate who has no spouse and yours is going, include an invitation for a guest, but not a specific guest.

Today's etiquette allows peers—men and women—to invite each other to social functions. If the invitation will be extended by phone, it's often easier for nonworking spouses or spouses with less hectic schedules to call on behalf of the couple, but this is no longer a requirement of social etiquette. It seems much friendlier for the people who know each other to make and accept invitations (after checking with their spouses, of course).

How to Address Invitations

Men:	Messeurs or Messrs. duPont, Disend, Bradley, and Alexander Messrs. Jim Smith and James Jones Mr. James Jones and Mr. Jim Smith
Women:	
Married:	Mesdames or Mmes., or separate names as above (with Mrs.)
Single:	Misses or Msses., or separate names as above (with Miss)
In general:	Mses., or separate names as above (with Ms.)
Male and female with different names (even if married):	Use two lines, with the man's name on the bottom line, or add *and* or a slash and use one line: Ms. Bertha Brown Mr. Wallace Wilder Ms. Bertha Brown and Mr. Wallace Wilder Ms. Bertha Brown/Mr. Wallace Wilder Dr. Phyllis Physician and Mr. Fred Herman For more than two: Mr. T. T. Jones, Ms. L. C. White, Ms. M. K. duPont or on one line each

Here's a list of other courtesy titles and how to write them:

Attorney:	Jane R. Black, Esquire (or Esq. or J.D.) Ms. Jane R. Blake, Attorney at Law
State Attorney, Judge, Mayor, Governor, Cabinet Member, Congressperson, Senator, Representative:	The Honorable J. J. Jay
President:	The President
General:	General (or Gen.) George Patton, USAF (USMC, USN, etc.)

Ambassador:	The Honorable J. J. Jay Ambassador to Mexico	(or American Ambassador)
	Her Excellency Juanita Rodriguez Ambassador to the U.S.	(or Mexican Ambassador)
Chief Justice:	The Chief Justice of the United States	
Consul, Consul General, Vice Consul:	Mr. William Stick, Esq. American Consul Paris, France	
	The Honorable Chu Sumu Chinese Consul Washington, DC 20001	
Professor:	Professor A. B. Galen, Ph.D. Dr. A. B. Galen	
Minister:	The Reverend Billy Graham The Reverend Dr. Graham	
Priest:	The Reverend Graham Thomas The Reverend Dr. Thomas The Reverend Father Graham Thomas The Reverend Father Thomas	
Rabbi:	Rabbi Jacob Stein	
Cardinal in the U.S.:	His Eminence Emanuel Syne His Eminence Cardinal Syne	
Mother Superior:	The Reverend Mother Superior Reverend Mother May Jane Smith Mother Mary Jane Smith, Superior	
Sister:	Sister May Jane Smith, RSCJ Sister Mary Jane Smith, SC	

RESPONDING TO INVITATIONS

Although you might make a greater effort to attend your manager's or an important client's social affair than you would for that of a coworker or supplier, your decision should never be reflected in your response. Timing and correctness should always be the same.

The most important letters in the etiquette of invitations are RSVP. RSVP does not mean "Let us know if you're coming." It means, "Let us know either way." Failure to reply to an invitation is a definite blunder (unless you've somehow contributed money for the invitation). Of course if the invitation specifies "Regrets only," you needn't acknowledge acceptance, but you do need to let the host know if you cannot make it.

Informal and oral invitations may be handled with less formality, but meeting your host in the hallway and saying, "Hey, thanks for the invitation. We'll be there!" does not constitute an RSVP. To respond to an informal invitation, either call the host or write a personal note.

When you are responding to a formal invitation, accept or decline in writing on personal stationery—unless you are using an RSVP card. Include the wording used in the invitation and state clearly whether you will or will not be attending. You do not need to explain in detail why you are declining. Always use a stamp (preferably an attractive commemorative), never a meter imprint. Your response may be made either one-to-one or couple-to-couple. If your invitation includes a guest, give the full name of the person attending with you and their relationship to you.

Example of Acceptance

Mr. and Mrs. Herman LaCross accept with pleasure your kind invitation for dinner on Saturday, November 5, at 8:00 P.M.

Example of Regret

Mrs. Elaine Goodrich and Mr. Jack Ortiz regret that a previous engagement prevents their accepting your kind invitation for dinner on Saturday, November 5, at 8:00 P.M.

Respond to any invitation—formal or informal—within 24 hours if possible (three days maximum). Your host is investing both money and time, and will appreciate being able to plan accurately. If you are uncertain whether you will be able to attend, let the host know immediately, and tell him or her when you will be able to respond, so as not to interfere with the event's arrangement.

Never cancel an acceptance for any reason other than an urgent one. If you absolutely must cancel, make the call or write the note yourself; don't ask someone else to do it for you. It's equally rude to send someone in your place if you have agreed to be there, and to bring uninvited guests.

If you are away and will not be back in time to return the RSVP, your assistant may phone the host or return the RSVP card. If you know the host well, your assistant should include a note with the RSVP, explaining your absence: "Ms. duPont is unable to respond herself because she is out of town on a business trip and won't return until after your dinner party. She asked me to thank you for your thoughtful invitation."

Just as the letters *RSVP* are magic, the word "Thanks" is also magic. Thank-you notes don't need to be long, but they do need to be sent for any event hosted by another. Any lapse of time over 48 hours is unforgivable.

Of course there are always office events that don't require an RSVP because they are command performances—the summer picnic, the holiday party. Should you go? Probably. Should you drink? Probably not. Should you stay long? No. Go, have a good time, and be seen. Shake hands, raise your cola for the toasts, and dance with the manager or the manager's spouse if you want. But, for the sake of your future, wear your best party or play clothes, or your least revealing evening clothes; don't talk too loudly or too much; and ignore the mistletoe.

DON'T GO EMPTY-HANDED

If you're invited to an event honoring someone—a wedding, christening, bas or bar mitzvah, anniversary party, and so on—a gift is definitely in order, even if you can't attend. The value of the gift should not be affected by your ability or inability to attend. If you don't receive a thank-you within 90 days, call and ask whether the gift was received. If the event is called off, you should expect to receive your gift back. If the event is for you, send flowers to the hostess before the party.

House gifts are customary when you attend a dinner party, open house, or similar function—especially at holiday time. The gift doesn't have to be expensive—a bag of flavored coffee, a loaf of homemade bread—but it does need to be handed to the host or hostess on arrival. Don't urge your host or hostess to open it, however, unless it's something that concerns the entire party. If you want to share in their delight with the gift, leave it unwrapped. Put a festive bow on the gift, or buy something in a decorative container.

You may personally deliver your gifts (especially liquor), or send them by mail or courier, preferably to the recipient's home. Personal delivery always seems much warmer, but personally delivering a business gift to an individual's home is inappropriate unless you've been invited there for a specific occasion.

Always include a note with the gift, handwritten on notepaper or a greeting card (not your business card), and in an envelope.

A gift is not required if you don't attend. You'll be thoughtful and proper, however, by sending flowers or a bottle of champagne to the house the day of, or the day before, the dinner party. Send a brief note with the gift, such as "We hope you and your guests have a delightful evening." The note should not refer to your lack of attendance.

Tasteful gifts to consider:

- A gold or silver pen
- Flowers or plants (yes, a woman may send flowers to a man!)
- An attractive appointment book or calendar
- An engraved key ring
- An elegant bookmark
- A basket of gourmet coffees, teas, cheeses, or fruit
- A bottle of champagne, or a favorite wine or liquor
- Pressurized balls for a tennis player
- Lures, tackle box, or other gear for a fishing enthusiast
- Special key holder or timepiece for a jogger
- Goggles, gloves, or hat for a skier
- Odometer or bike gloves for a cyclist

Gifts you should never give:

- Anything overly expensive
- Perfumed stationery
- Anything smutty, sarcastic, sexual, or extremely personal
- Animals
- Liquor to nondrinkers, candy to dieters, etc.
- Clothing (wallets and handbags are acceptable)
- Anything oversized or fragile to someone who has to fly with it
- Perfume or cologne unless you know their preferred fragrance
- Anything of inferior quality

EXERCISE

Answer True or False. For those you answer as false, what is the correct answer?

	True	False
1. You don't have to send a wedding present if you don't plan to attend the wedding.	❏	❏
2. A woman should never send flowers to a man unless he's hospitalized.	❏	❏
3. It's rude to return a gift.		
4. You don't have to send thank-you notes to close friends.	❏	❏
5. You don't have to thank people for a party at their house if you took a gift.	❏	❏
6. When your manager invites you for lunch or dinner, you must reciprocate.	❏	❏
7. RSVP means "regrets only."	❏	❏
8. Invitations to a formal dinner may be handwritten.	❏	❏
9. A gift certificate is the perfect answer in business gift giving.	❏	❏

Answers on page 109.

SECTION

IX

Multicultural Etiquette

MULTICULTURAL ETIQUETTE

The United States is very much a multicultural society. Immigrants are arriving at the rate of more than 1 million a year. Today, more than 20 million American residents were born in another country. The 1990 census showed 300 distinct cultures in the United States, and each of them has a different view of what's proper etiquette—based on their upbringing and cultural traditions. Confusing, yes, but wouldn't it be a boring world if we were all just alike?

Defining the Challenge

The problem is, of course, that while differences in people are important and rewarding, they are also challenging. Sometimes it's hard to recognize one nationality from another. Certain people may not react when you speak to them or perform in the way you expect, and that may make you uncomfortable. What moves you doesn't seem to motivate them in the same way, and that may cause you to question their motives.

Unfortunately, our business dealings with coworkers and customers are often swift and impersonal, so we don't have much time to analyze or try to figure out how they would like to be treated. At the very least, we must remember that all people want to feel valued, respected, heard, and understood. They don't always expect a "yes," but they always expect an "I'll try." They all want you to provide the product, service, or behavior you promised, in a way that is respectful and personal. They want you to quickly and efficiently solve any problems that arise and apologize if something goes wrong.

This challenge is compounded when our customers, managers, or employees are from a culture that is different from our own.

Examples:

- Say you compliment a coworker on a piece of clothing. When this happens to most Americans, they beam from ear to ear. But an Asian may quickly divert her eyes and murmur softly. Then she hurries away. How will this affect your view of her? Will you be more understanding if you realize that, for many people from the Asian culture, accepting praise in front of others is a sign of being vain?

MULTICULTURAL ETIQUETTE (continued)

- You have a meeting with a Middle Easterner and are running late. You would likely be concerned about that and might be frustrated and upset when you finally arrive. How would you feel if you were then kept waiting another 30–40 minutes? To Americans, time is power. To many other cultures, time has less significance. Many from the Middle Eastern culture believe everything comes in its own time, whenever that is.

Ultimately, protocol is a matter of perception. Unfortunately, it's others' perception of your words and actions that define the experience to them. Because each person's needs and feelings are different, protocol can't be a "cookie cutter" behavior. Each interaction must be tailored to the person you're dealing with at that moment. I hope this section will make you aware of the differences in cultural etiquette and how the people you work with and serve would like to be treated.

Using Names Correctly

One of the areas where we have protocol problems is the names we use for people. We don't usually mean to offend others by what we call them; we just don't know any better. And sometimes even the group itself doesn't agree on what they prefer to be called. As a rule, however, *Asian* has displaced *Oriental*, *Native American* has superseded *American Indian*, and *African American* has replaced *Black*. Rather than the all-inclusive *Hispanic American*, some Hispanics prefer the *American* suffix attached to their actual country of origin (*Latin American, Mexican American, Chilean American*, etc.), and some prefer simply *Latino/Latina* or *Chicano/Chicana*. Many Native Americans feel the same way; they would prefer to be known by their individual tribe's name.

Personal names may also be confusing. Many countries have different rules for individuals' names than America does, and Americans should honor the person's wishes. Age also plays a part in what to call people, even in America. Many of the "older" generation still prefer the titles "Mr." and "Mrs." In some other cultures, younger people must show respect by using the titles "Aunt" and "Uncle" for older people, even if the younger person is 90! This tradition has been practiced in Africa for many generations, and many African Americans continue it in their homes. Whenever you are unsure how to address someone, the most polite thing to do is *ask first!*

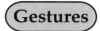

Gestures

Many gestures can seem like a breach of good manners. Nonverbals are usually readily understood within our own culture but may easily be misinterpreted by people from other cultures, no matter how long they've lived in the United States. It's true that actions often speak louder than words, and no gestures are universal. In addition, body language is more important to many people from other cultures than it is to most Americans. The way that words are said, and the hand movements, posture, and facial expressions that accompany words, often have greater significance than the words themselves. In addition, the less English that people understand, the more they will tend to rely on body language.

Giving the typical American gesture for *OK,* for instance, would likely be perceived as poor manners by someone from France, Belgium, or Tunisia, where that same gesture signifies *worthless* or *zero.* In many other countries, the American *OK* sign represents an obscene or lewd comment.

People sometimes use inappropriate gestures without even knowing it. We fold our arms, stand in a certain position, move our body in a way that might be considered provocative or rude by others, or make eye contact when we shouldn't. Business travelers in particular need to be alert for behavior that could offend a host or doom a deal.

Examples:

- To beckon the attention of someone, Americans might whistle, use a crooked finger, or wave frantically—palm out, fingers up, in a horizontal movement. Waving like this is deeply offensive to Mexican, Filipino, Vietnamese, Taiwan, and French people. It's often the way people call prostitutes, animals, or "inferior" people! In Taiwan, the correct way to get someone's attention is to wave your hand, palm down, in a way that looks like the Western signal to go away. Middle Easterners prefer the right hand out, palm up, with an open and closing movement (like the American "give me some" gesture). For some other cultures, a better way is to use the vertical wave Americans use to say good-bye.

- Even how you shake your head to indicate "yes" or "no" may differ significantly from culture to culture. Americans might understand something totally different when Bulgarians shake their head from side to side. Their way of saying "yes" would look like "no" in the United States.

MULTICULTURAL ETIQUETTE (continued)

- Something as simple as how we sit may send an unintended message. For instance, the open way American men cross their legs while sitting sometimes offends Europeans. For the more formal Europeans, this behavior expresses crudeness. Most Asians and Middle Easterners also regard crossing the legs to be in poor taste. One of the reasons for this is that, when the legs are crossed, the bottom of the foot is showing and the toe is pointing at someone—both of which are considered offensive. Iranians feel it is inappropriate to stretch the legs out in front of you.

Touch

Americans like to touch, kiss, embrace, take people by the arm, pat them on the back. In many other countries, this behavior is totally inappropriate, particularly in business. Chinese do not like body contact with strangers at all, even a quick pat. They, like other Asians, are particularly offended by a touch on the back, head, or shoulder (even children). It's also inappropriate to put your arm on the back of a chair in which an Asian is sitting. In general, keep touch to a severe minimum when doing business with people from other cultures. And, unlike Americans, who find it unusual for people of the same sex to hold hands, it is a perfectly acceptable sign of nonromantic friendship for Asians, Latinos, Middle Easterners, and the French, so don't be surprised or make comments about it.

Business Cards

Americans treat business cards as objects, throwing them into a pocket or purse without even glancing at them. The Chinese, on the other hand, take cards very seriously and are prepared to exchange business cards early in a meeting. The Japanese exchange cards often and with everyone in the room. With Asian coworkers, however, don't offer your card until asked, or you may appear too aggressive. When you give your card to an Asian, present it with both hands, and make sure the type is facing the recipient, right side up. When you receive a card from an Asian at the same time you are presenting yours, take it with your right hand and give yours with your left hand. If you are sitting at a desk, put the person's card in front of you on the desk until the meeting is over. Never present a business card with your left hand to people from Southeast Asia, Africa, or the Middle East (except Israel).

Eye Contact

Typically, Americans are taught that the more eye contact they give, the more power they are perceived to have, and that if someone doesn't give enough eye contact, something is wrong. In many cultures, however, especially Asian, less eye contact is more respectful. Also in many other cultures, females will be less inclined than males to look another person in the eye. It confuses many Americans when their employees, managers, or customers don't give them the contact they are expecting. They begin to think that the other person is doing something they are ashamed of. Jumping to these conclusions can harm your business relationships. Make sure you understand the other person's culture and background before you become suspicious.

If, however, you are dealing with a nonnative who is not making strong eye contact, don't alter your usual way of communicating. Other cultures expect Americans to make eye contact. They do not, of course, want or expect you to stare or continue to look closely at them if they are visibly embarrassed.

Smiling

Americans usually smile to show pleasure and good nature, but that's not true of all cultures. The importance of a smile and the fine points of timing vary from culture to culture.

Examples:

- For Middle Easterners, a smile might be used to placate someone, thus avoiding conflict.

- To smile at a French person on the street is considered an inappropriate intrusion.

- Many nonnatives use a smile to acknowledge a message that has not truly been understood.

- Japanese usually will not smile at serious events, including getting a driver's license (it would show frivolity for a serious responsibility).

- Asians generally may smile when they are happy, sad, apologetic, angry, frustrated, disagreeing, thankful, or even confused.

MULTICULTURAL ETIQUETTE (continued)

Personal Space

Getting too close to some people can offend them if they are not comfortable with tight personal space. Have you ever walked up to someone and had them back away from you? Perhaps their culture doesn't like having people that close to them, while your culture likes to get up close and personal. So there is a feeling of conflict, and neither of you may be consciously aware that conversational distance or personal space is an issue.

Most Americans have a personal space of 18 inches to three feet; in a business setting, they don't like having others closer than a couple of feet. With strangers, Americans tend to want even more distance. They try to leave an empty seat between them and a stranger if at all possible; they dislike the center seat on airplanes, buses, and cars. They become uncomfortable if an elevator gets too crowded. What Americans don't realize is that, in those cultures in which physical closeness is more comfortable, it can be considered an insult to stand so far away and to leave that seat empty.

Western Europeans have the same comfort zone as most Americans—18 inches to three feet, but Middle Easterners who are of the same sex, Mediterraneans, and some Hispanic cultures are comfortable with a personal distance of less than 18 inches—an in-your-face type of communication. Most of the rest of the world—Asians, many African cultures, Middle Eastern men with women—prefer more than three feet of personal space.

For more on multicultural norms, read M. Kay duPont's book *Handling Diversity in the Workplace: Communication is the Key*, published by American Media, Inc.

EXERCISE

Answer True or False. For those you answer as false, what is the correct answer?

	True	False
1. All cultures appreciate brevity and succinctness, especially in writing.	❑	❑
2. Saying "please" and "thank you" is still good practice.	❑	❑
3. A strong handshake is always an acceptable greeting.	❑	❑
4. The American thumbs-up always means "good job."	❑	❑
5. Rubbing your thumb and forefinger together always signifies that something costs, or pays, money.	❑	❑
6. An up-and-down head nod always means "yes."	❑	❑
7. Crossing your fingers is how everyone symbolizes a wish for good luck.	❑	❑
8. Patting a child on the head is always a compliment.	❑	❑
9. Pointing at someone is normally considered rude.	❑	❑

Answers on page 110.

X

Summary and Answers to Exercises

ETIQUOTE

Work spares us from three great evils: boredom, vice, and need.

—Voltaire
Candide

SUMMARY

One way to become what you want to be, whatever you choose, is to study the people who are that way. About 20 years ago, I became dissatisfied with my lifestyle. I was not very professional or successful (in my eyes, at least). My mother, who's a very wise woman, said, "Kay, if you want to be successful, you have to hang around with successful people." So I began to associate with and study people who were strong, who were successful. I wanted to know what made them that way.

You can do the same thing. If you know someone who is professional and tactfully assertive—someone who has the attributes, characteristics, skills, and good manners described in this book—study that person. When you see people you think are really top-notch, get to know those people. Watch what they do—how they act. Ask yourself, "What clothing do they have on, how do they walk, how do they talk, what is their voice like, what did they just say or do that intimidated or impressed me?" You can start your learning process just by imitating those you respect.

But please don't take these rules of business etiquette (or any other social rules) too seriously. Socializing with others—like life itself—is supposed to be enjoyable. Enjoyment is extremely important to your professional life, your personal life, and your career success.

Research at major universities has identified several characteristics associated with high achievers—people who get the things they want. These people are happy and balanced in their mental, emotional, physical, financial, and spiritual lives. They continuously focus on, review, and refine their intellectual, physical, and emotional habits. They believe in both a higher being and a higher self. They possess a perspective and a sense of purpose that are not limited by time and space and "what used to be" or "what should be." With this dignified sense of self-worth, blended with balance and purpose, hard work and commitment, respect and kindness for others, these people achieve extraordinary things. But they are only ordinary people, just like you.

Good luck!

Kay

ANSWERS TO EXERCISE QUESTIONS

SECTION II (page 15)

1. False. Change the subject or say, without sarcasm, "I'd rather not discuss my personal life. You don't mind, do you?"

2. False. Never make passes at coworkers, don't pay personal compliments to strangers, and never berate your own company—no matter how long you've been there.

3. False. Accept the gift graciously, even if you didn't need (or want) the favor.

4. False. Never discuss anything confidential with your coworkers.

5. False. Coming to work late shows a lack of commitment and dedication; working through lunch shows that you weren't hungry.

6. False. You never get a second chance to make a first impression.

7. False. It's a two-way street, and each side has total responsibility for the communication.

8. False. Be even more reserved in the beginning. Give them time to get used to your presence before you start being the office charmer.

9. False. Most managers prefer to hear solutions, not problems. No one minds answering your questions in the beginning, or even helping you solve a few minor problems, but don't expect that help to last forever.

10. False. It's up to you to make yourself—and them—feel comfortable. Go out of your way to meet your new coworkers and make friends.

SECTION III (pages 31–32)

1. (b) Shake, but apologize about your hands, explaining that you've been drinking a cold drink.

2. (b) Ask again, because you don't want to alienate a potential associate.

3. (b) Stand up and offer your hand.

4. Either (a) rise and greet her if it's an unusual occasion or if she is much higher in rank, or (c) look up and greet her if it's a common occurrence.

5. (b) Tell him you'll be glad to tell the owner that he is there if you can tell the owner the nature of his business.

6. (a) The client's name.

7. Yes. It's always appropriate for either a man or a woman to initiate a handshake.

8. Immediately repeat the name out loud, and then repeat it to yourself several times. Associate the name and/or person with the person's hobbies, interests, or career.

9. Ten minutes.

SECTION IV (pages 43–44)

Scoring

Give yourself 4 points for *Always* answers; 2 points for *Usually;* 0 points for *Seldom.*

60–56 points: You have a winning telephone personality!
55–46 points: A little more effort will bring big rewards.
Below 46: Concentrate on forming better telephone habits, and try taking this test again.

SECTION V (page 55)

1. False. Unsolicited faxes cost the recipient paper and transmission time.

2. False. Send a separate fax to each person who needs one.

3. False. People like to know that they have reached the correct party.

4. False. Always leave your phone number; most people like to write it down as they listen to the message.

5. False. Always leave a message—even just to say you have reached a wrong number.

ANSWERS TO EXERCISE QUESTIONS (continued)

6. False. Nine out of 10 people hate voice mail.

7. False. Make it professional and short—20 seconds or less.

8. False. E-mail is more conversational than letters or faxes, so be informal but polite.

9. False. In the electronic world, all caps are the equivalent of SHOUTING!

10. False. Even if you don't have a full reply right then, acknowledge the receipt and let the other person know you'll be getting back to them.

SECTION VI (page 65)

1. False. The site should be determined by the theme and purpose of the meeting.

2. False. Stand out of respect, especially when the woman is a visitor, a higher-ranking person, a guest, or an older person.

3. False. It's better etiquette to separate them.

4. False. They need at least two weeks.

5. True.

6. False. That's one of the duties of a receptionist. He or she is not there, however, to wait on you or keep you company.

7. False. Wait for your host to indicate which seat you should take.

8. False. Keep your papers in your lap.

SECTION VII (page 81)

1. False. You may order a drink (preferably wine or beer, and only one) if you want it. And it's certainly all right to decline. It may even be better to order something soft, because you are representing both your company and your manager.

2. False. All wine glasses should be held by the stem, not the bowl. Only liquids that taste better warm (brandy, cognac, etc.) should be held by the bowl.

3. False. It's quite acceptable if your drink is very hot.

4. False. The highest-ranking person goes on your right.

5. False. Wait in the lobby, if possible. If there is no lobby, you may wait at the bar or at your table.

6. False. The host always pays (even if the host is a hostess).

7. False. The guests immediately follow the maitre d', with the host in the rear.

8. False. Always serve your guests first.

9. False. Tipping should be for good service. If the service was poor, the tip should be poor—or nonexistent.

10. False. Both may be eaten whole from your fork.

SECTION VIII (page 92)

1. False. Even if you do not attend, a gift is definitely in order.

2. False. Men like flowers too!

3. False. You may return it to the store for replacement or exchange, or you may return it to the giver if you think it would be inappropriate to keep it.

4. False. Even close friends deserve courtesy.

5. False. Thank-you notes are essential to good etiquette.

6. False, especially if your meal function was for business reasons.

7. False. It means "Let us know either way."

8. True. Or they may be engraved.

9. False. Although it's safe and easy, it's often considered impersonal by the recipient.

ANSWERS TO EXERCISE QUESTIONS (continued)

SECTION IX (page 101)

1. False. The American "bottom-line" style is offensive to relationship-oriented cultures.

2. True.

3. False. Although American etiquette demands that you shake hands with everyone—with no protocol except equality—there are many countries in which people do not shake hands at all. In many Asian countries, for example, body contact is considered disrespectful, so the accepted greeting is a nod or a bow and a verbal exchange. Many Asian workers may carry this belief and, even though intellectually they know differently, they may still feel that you're disrespecting them if you greet them with a firm handshake. When establishing relations with Asians, it's probably wise to avoid all body contact, unless they initiate it.

4. False. In Australia, it means "up yours"; in Germany, "one"; in Japan, "five"; in Saudi Arabia, "I'm winning"; in Ghana, it is an insult; and in Afghanistan and Nigeria, it is an obscene gesture.

5. False. In France, it means something is perfect; in the Mediterranean, it's a vulgar gesture.

6. False. In parts of the Middle East, India, and Pakistan, the head is shaken to indicate "yes" and nodded for "no." In the Philippines, the head is often moved downward to indicate "no," and the head and eyebrows will be raised for "yes." In the Middle East, sometimes the chin is held up slightly and a clicking sound is made for "no." However, most people who have been in America for any length of time have adopted American ways in this area.

7. False. In North America and parts of Europe, yes. But do it in Paraguay, and you're sure to offend.

8. False. In many parts of Asia, it will be interpreted as a curse on the child.

9. True. Pointing at people (and often at objects) is poor etiquette in most cultures, including America. In Asian cultures, all pointing is frowned on. If you must point, use your entire hand.

CRISP WORLDWIDE DISTRIBUTION

English language books are distributed worldwide. Major international distributors include:

ASIA/PACIFIC

Australia/New Zealand: In Learning, PO Box 1051, Springwood QLD, Brisbane, Australia 4127   Tel: 61-7-3-841-2286, Facsimile: 61-7-3-841-1580
ATTN: Messrs. Richard/Robert Gordon

Hong Kong/Mainland China: Crisp Learning Solutions, 18/F Honest Motors Building 9-11 Leighton Rd., Causeway Bay, Hong Kong   Tel: 852-2915-7119,
Facsimile: 852-2865-2815 ATTN: Ms. Grace Lee

Indonesia: Pt Lutan Edukasi, Citra Graha, 7th Floor, Suite 701A, Jl. Jend. Gato Subroto Kav. 35-36, Jakarta 12950 Indonesia Tel: 62-21-527-9060/527-9061
Facsimile: 62-21-527-9062 ATTN: Mr. Suwardi Luis

Japan: Phoenix Associates, Believe Mita Bldg., 8th Floor 3-43-16 Shiba, Minato-ku, Tokyo 105-0014, Japan   Tel: 81-3-5427-6231, Facsimile: 81-3-5427-6232
ATTN: Mr. Peter Owans

Malaysia, Philippines, Singapore: Epsys Pte Ltd., 540 Sims Ave #04-01, Sims Avenue Centre, 387603, Singapore   Tel: 65-747-1964, Facsimile: 65-747-0162 ATTN: Mr. Jack Chin

CANADA

Crisp Learning Canada, 60 Briarwood Avenue, Mississauga, ON L5G 3N6 Canada
Tel: 905-274-5678, Facsimile: 905-278-2801 ATTN: Mr. Steve Connolly

EUROPEAN UNION

England: Flex Learning Media, Ltd., 9-15 Hitchin Street,
Baldock, Hertfordshire, SG7 6AL, England
Tel: 44-1-46-289-6000, Facsimile: 44-1-46-289-2417   ATTN: Mr. David Willetts

INDIA

Multi-Media HRD, Pvt. Ltd., National House, Floor 1, 6 Tulloch Road,
Appolo Bunder, Bombay, India 400-039 Tel: 91-22-204-2281,
Facsimile: 91-22-283-6478 ATTN: Messrs. Ajay Aggarwal/ C.L. Aggarwal

SOUTH AMERICA

Mexico: Grupo Editorial Iberoamerica, Nebraska 199, Col. Napoles, 03810 Mexico, D.F.
Tel: 525-523-0994, Facsimile: 525-543-1173   ATTN: Señor Nicholas Grepe

SOUTH AFRICA

Corporate: Learning Resources, PO Box 2806, Parklands, Johannesburg 2121, South Africa, Tel: 27-21-531-2923, Facsimile: 27-21-531-2944 ATTN: Mr. Ricky Robinson

MIDDLE EAST

Edutech Middle East, L.L.C., PO Box 52334, Dubai U.A.E.
Tel: 971-4-359-1222, Facsimile: 971-4-359-6500   ATTN: Mr. A.S.F. Karim